George Washington Carver

written by **Joeming Dunn**
illustrated by **Chris Allen**

Published by Magic Wagon, a division of the ABDO Publishing Group, 8000 West 78th Street, Edina, Minnesota 55439. Copyright © 2009 by Abdo Consulting Group, Inc. International copyrights reserved in all countries. All rights reserved. No part of this book may be reproduced in any form without written permission from the publisher.
Graphic Planet™ is a trademark and logo of MagicWagon.

Printed in the United States.

Written by Joeming Dunn
Illustrated by Chris Allen
Edited by Stephanie Hedlund and Rochelle Baltzer
Interior layout and design by Antarctic Press
Cover art by Chris Allen and Rod Espinosa
Cover design by Neil Klinepier

Library of Congress Cataloging-in-Publication Data

Dunn, Joeming W.
    George Washington Carver / written by Joeming Dunn ; illustrated by Chris Allen.
    p. cm. -- (Bio-graphics)
  Includes index.
  ISBN 978-1-60270-171-7
    1. Carver, George Washington, 1864?-1943--Juvenile literature. 2. African American agriculturists--Biography--Juvenile literature. 3. Agriculturists--United States--Biography--Juvenile literature. I. Allen, Chris, 1972- ill. II. Title.

S417.C3.D86 2008
630.92--dc22
[B]   2007051479

TABLE of CONTENTS

Timeline

1864 – George Washington Carver was born near Diamond Grove, Missouri.

1890 – Carver attended Simpson College in Iowa.

1896 – Carver earned master's degree from Iowa State College; Carver became director of agriculture at Tuskegee Normal and Industrial Institute.

1921 – Carver spoke to the U.S. Congress about the importance of peanuts.

1923 – Carver was awarded the Springarn Medal by the National Association for the Advancement of Colored People (NAACP).

1943 – George Washington Carver died on January 5.

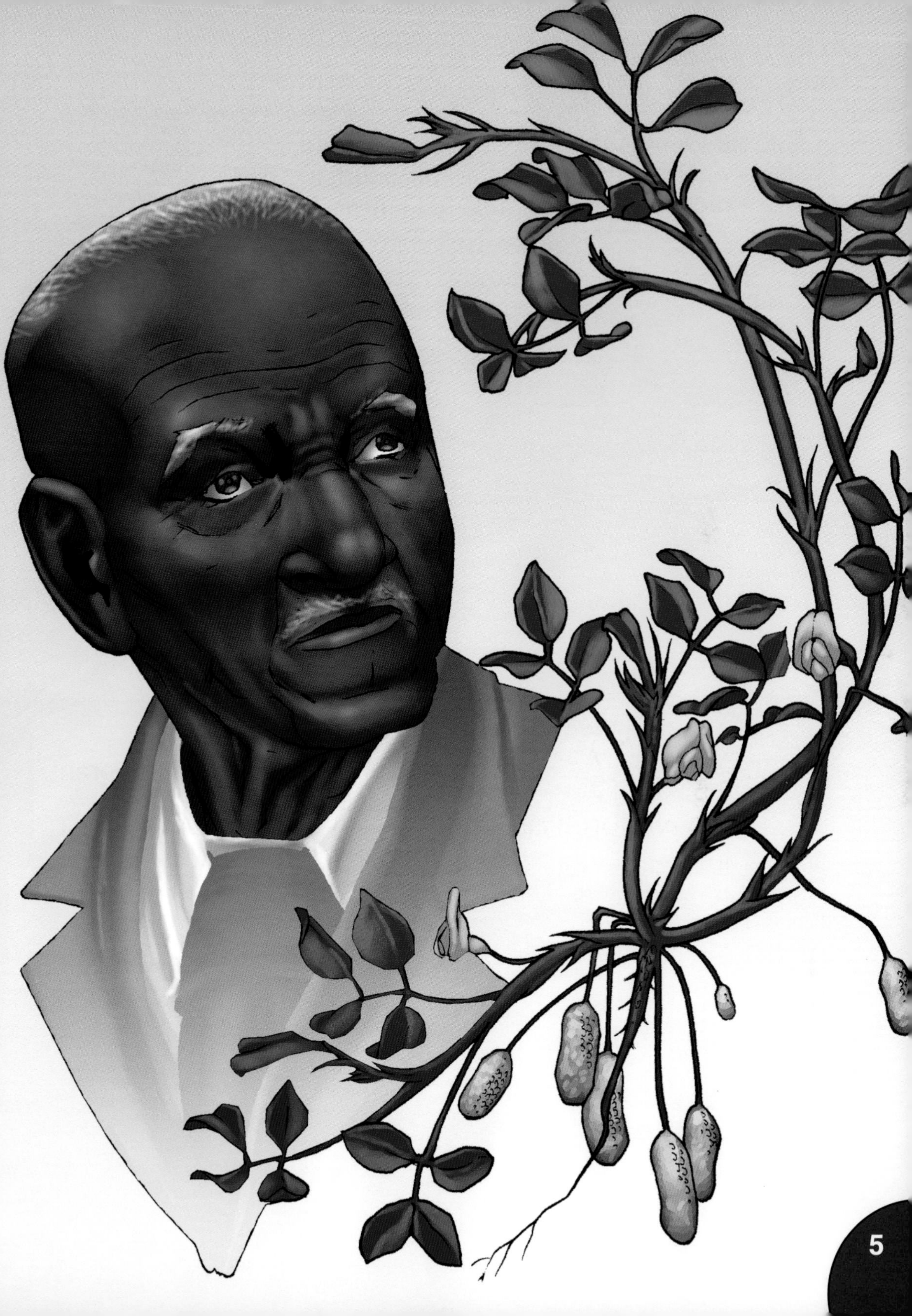

Chapter 1 Young Plant Doctor

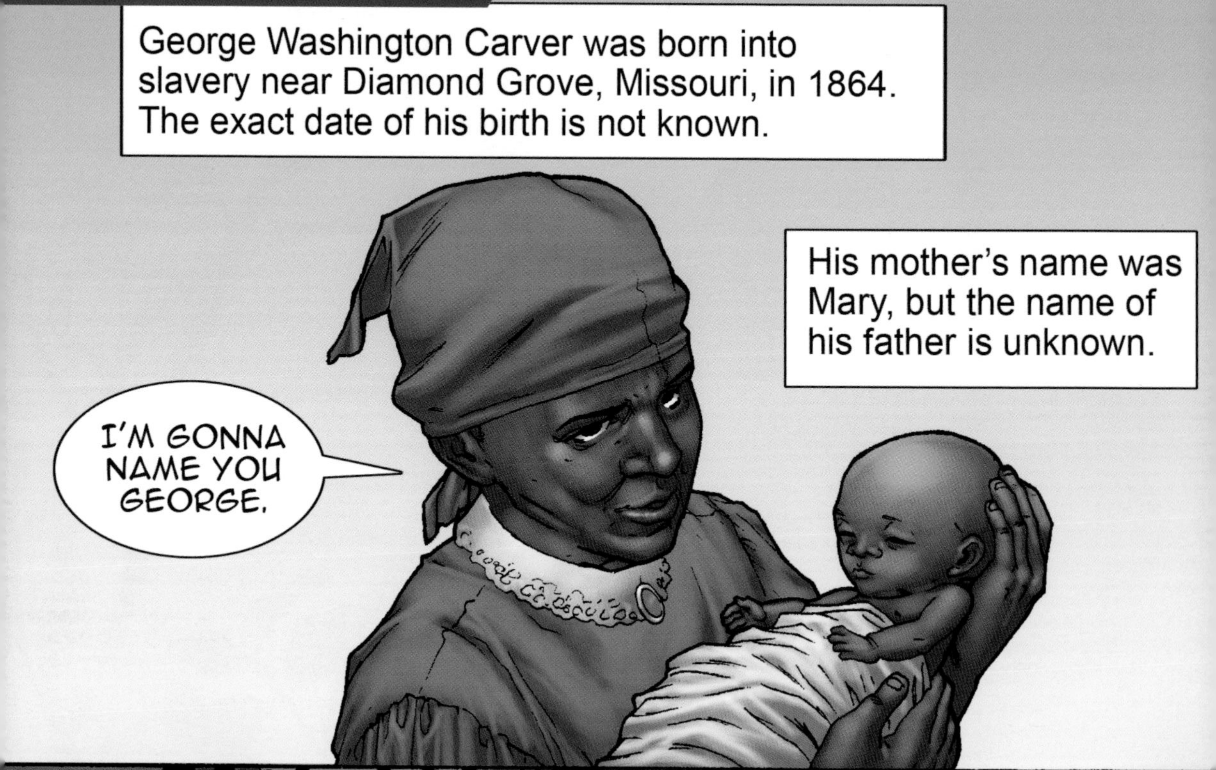
George Washington Carver was born into slavery near Diamond Grove, Missouri, in 1864. The exact date of his birth is not known.
His mother's name was Mary, but the name of his father is unknown.
I'M GONNA NAME YOU GEORGE.

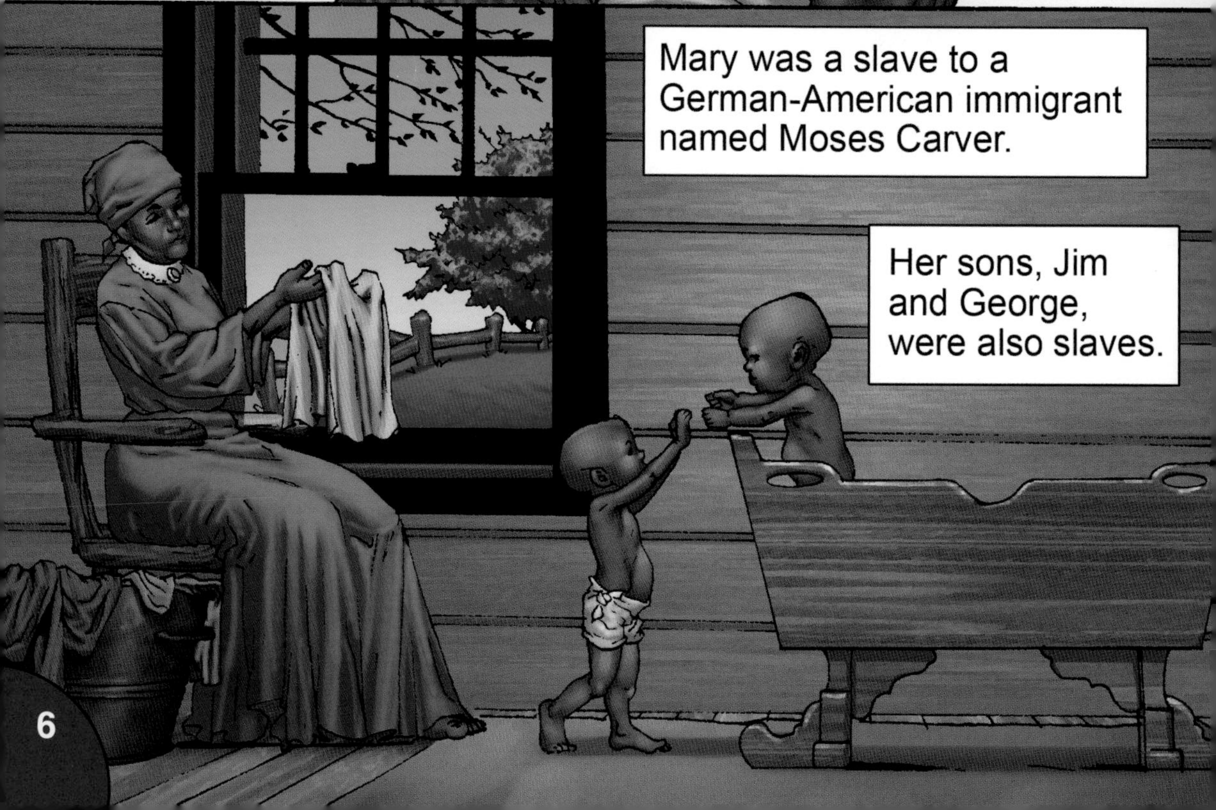
Mary was a slave to a German-American immigrant named Moses Carver.
Her sons, Jim and George, were also slaves.

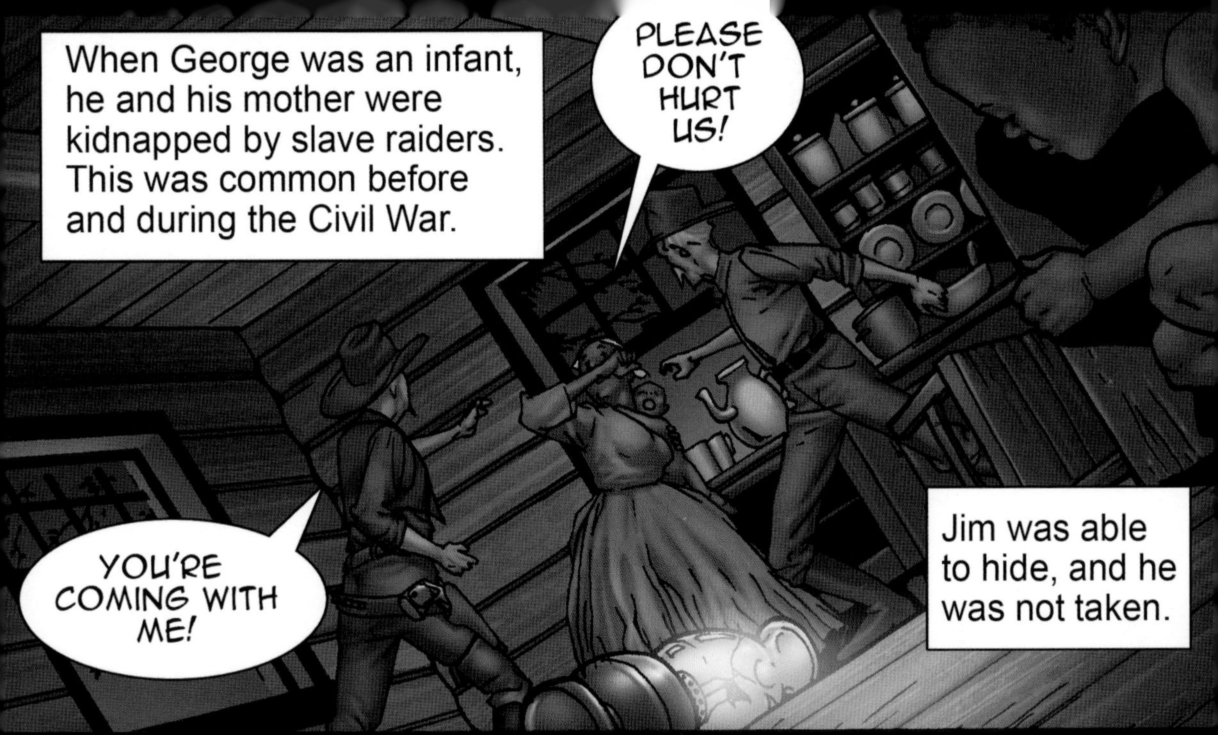
When George was an infant, he and his mother were kidnapped by slave raiders. This was common before and during the Civil War.
PLEASE DON'T HURT US!
YOU'RE COMING WITH ME!
Jim was able to hide, and he was not taken.

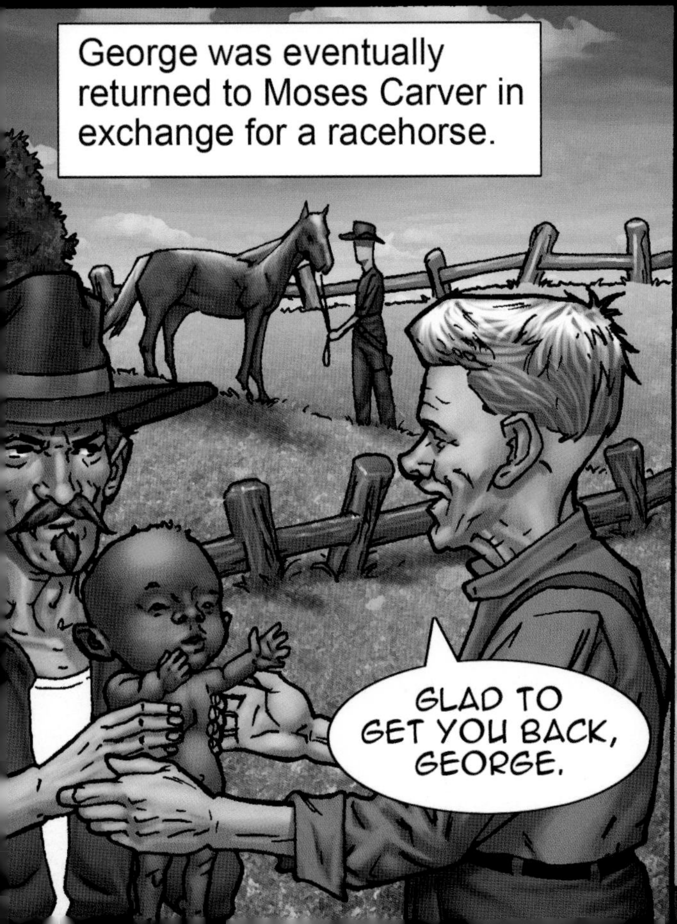
George was eventually returned to Moses Carver in exchange for a racehorse.
GLAD TO GET YOU BACK, GEORGE.

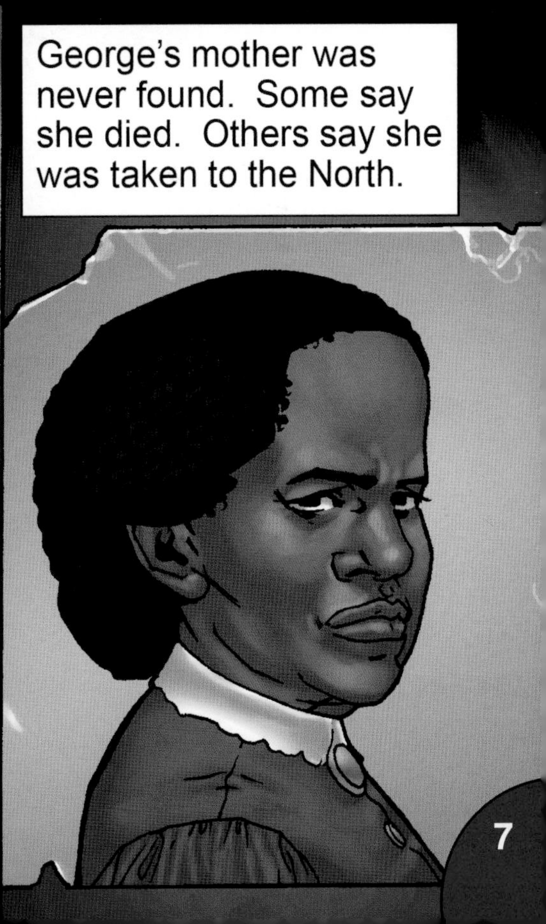
George's mother was never found. Some say she died. Others say she was taken to the North.

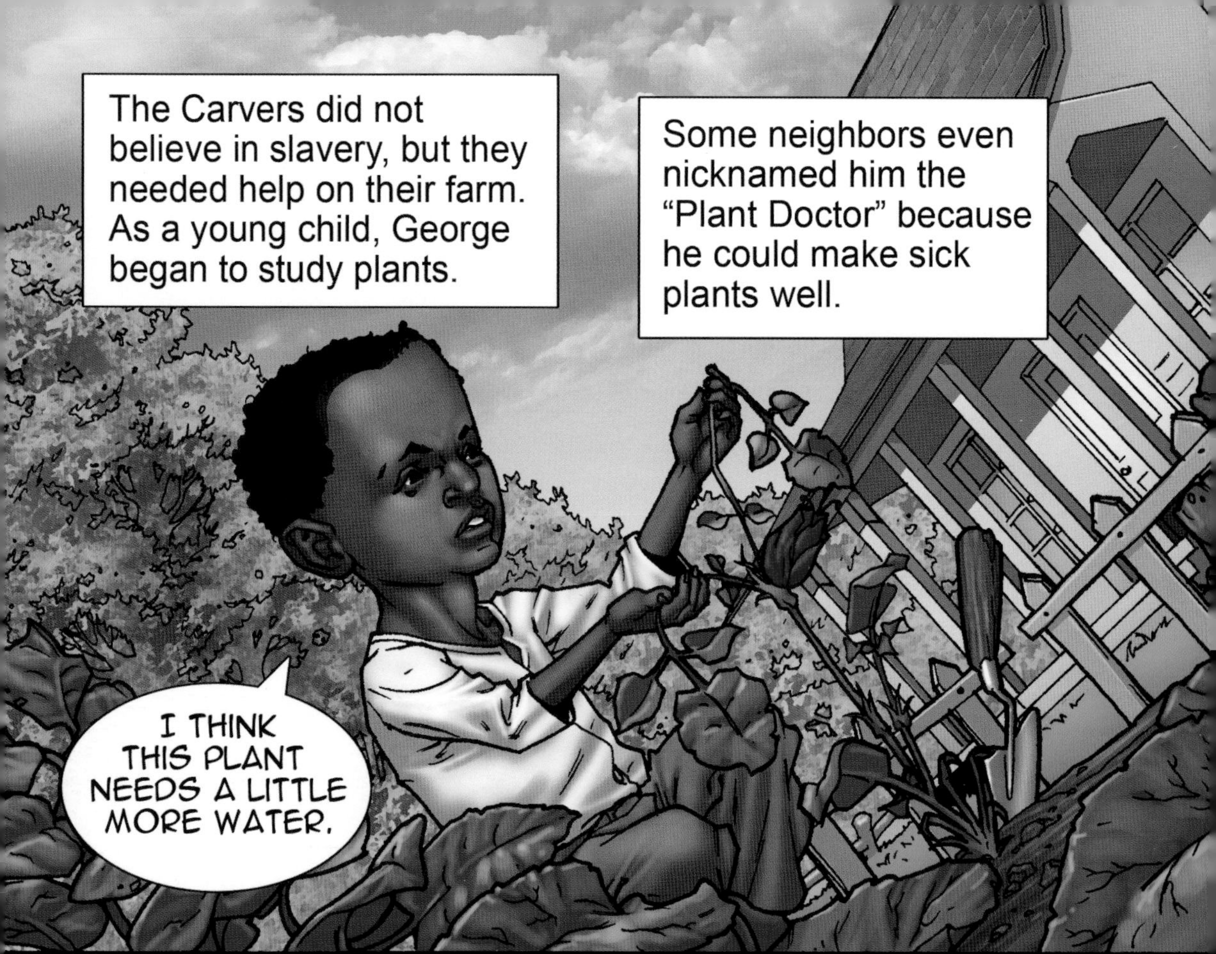

The Carvers did not believe in slavery, but they needed help on their farm. As a young child, George began to study plants.
Some neighbors even nicknamed him the "Plant Doctor" because he could make sick plants well.
I THINK THIS PLANT NEEDS A LITTLE MORE WATER.

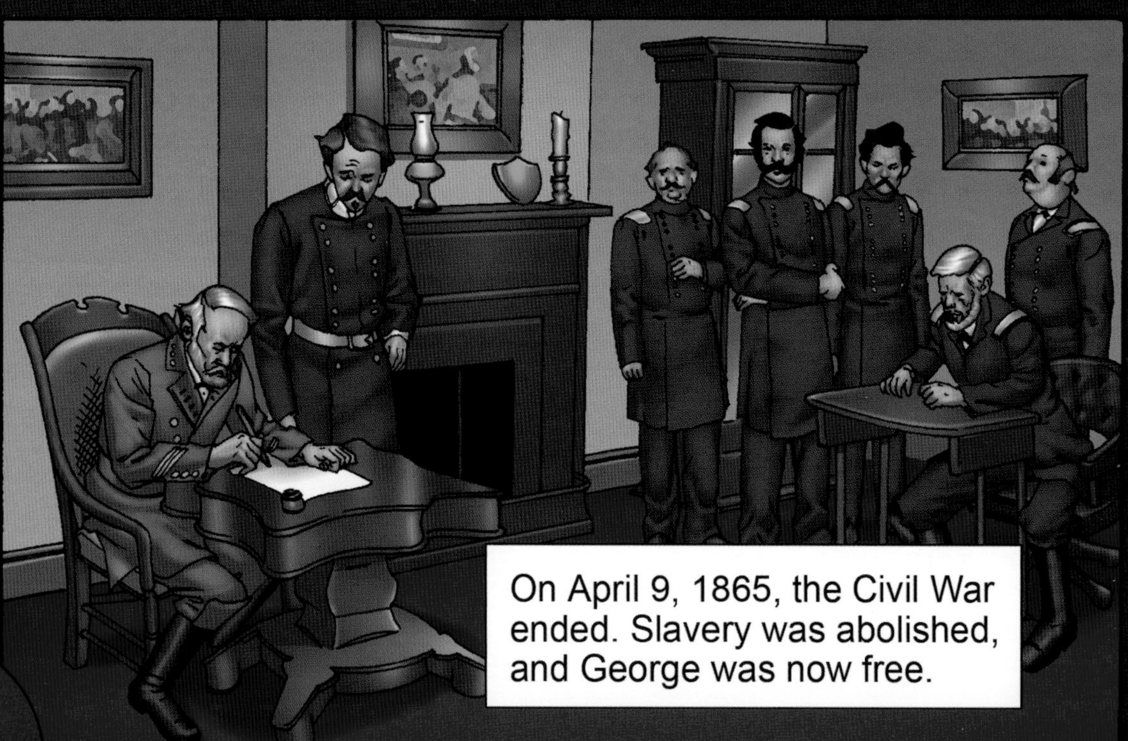

On April 9, 1865, the Civil War ended. Slavery was abolished, and George was now free.

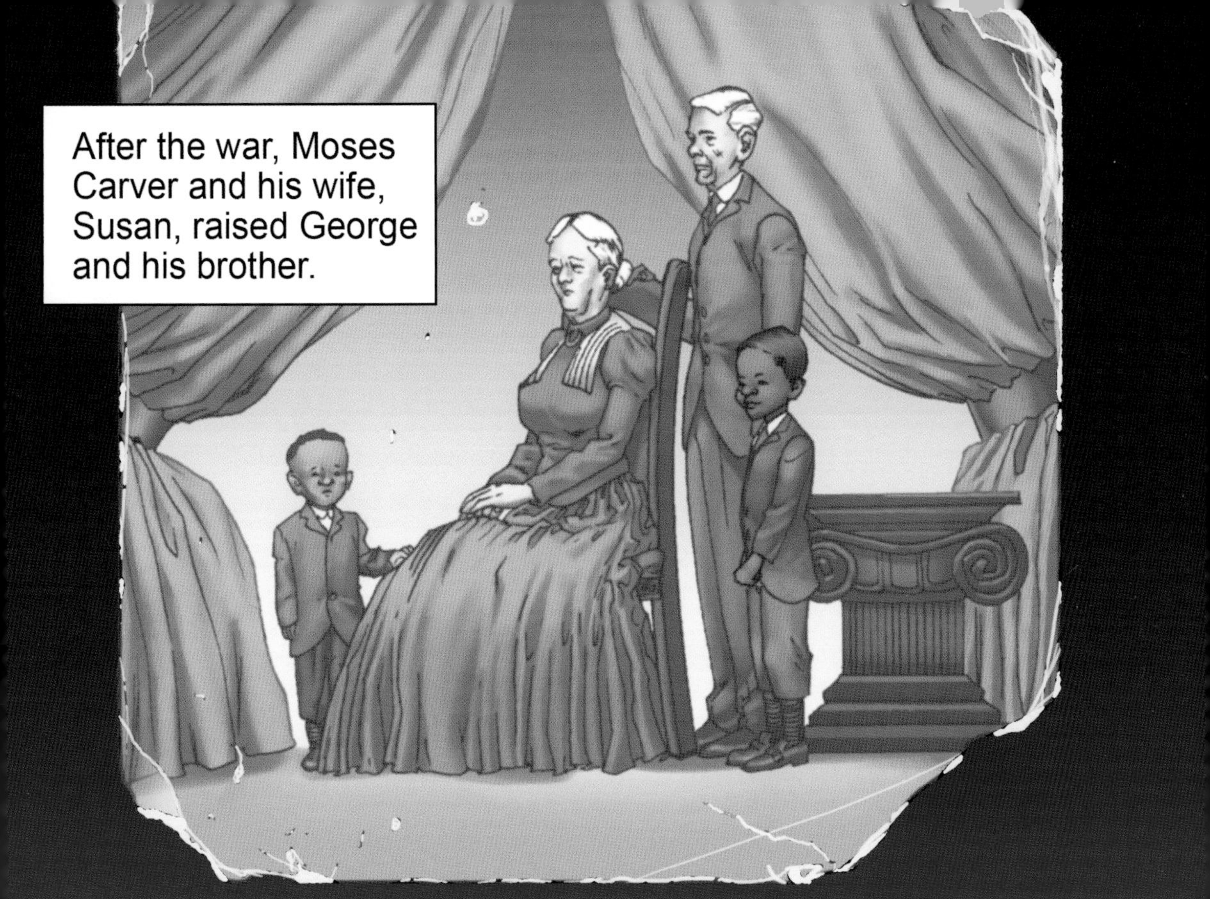
After the war, Moses Carver and his wife, Susan, raised George and his brother.

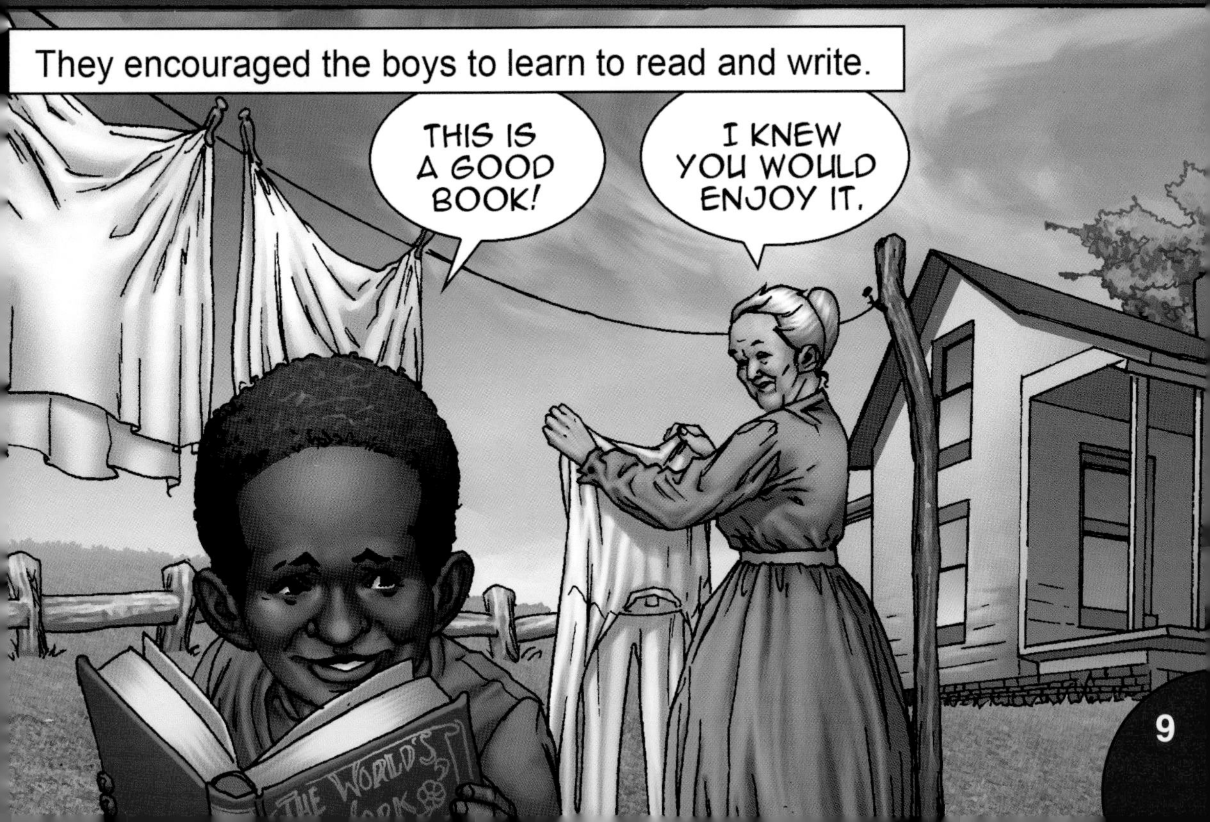
They encouraged the boys to learn to read and write.
THIS IS A GOOD BOOK!
I KNEW YOU WOULD ENJOY IT.
THE WORLD'S

Chapter 2 Fighting for an Education

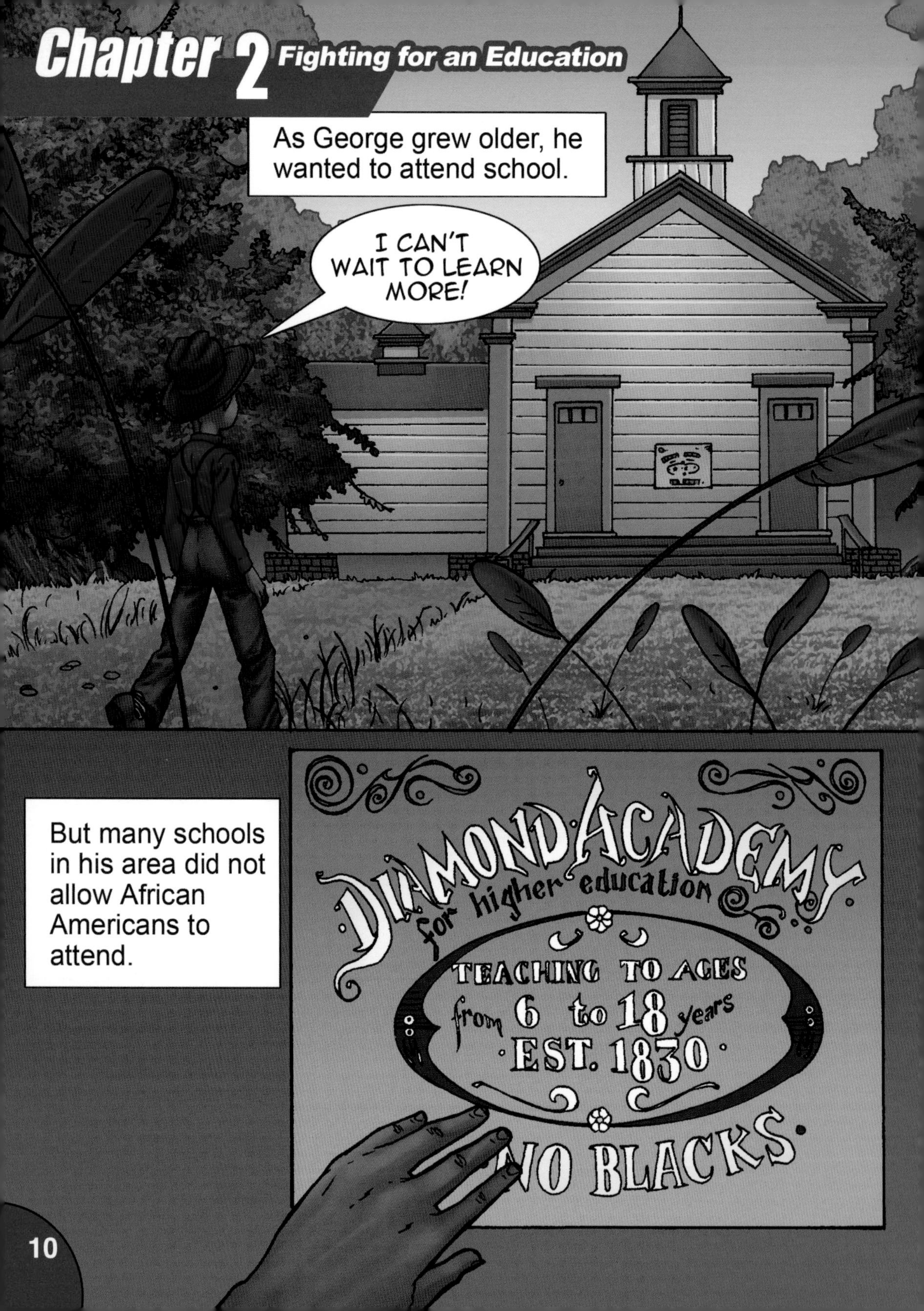
As George grew older, he wanted to attend school.
I CAN'T WAIT TO LEARN MORE!
But many schools in his area did not allow African Americans to attend.
DIAMOND ACADEMY
for higher education
TEACHING TO AGES from 6 to 18 years
EST. 1830
NO BLACKS.

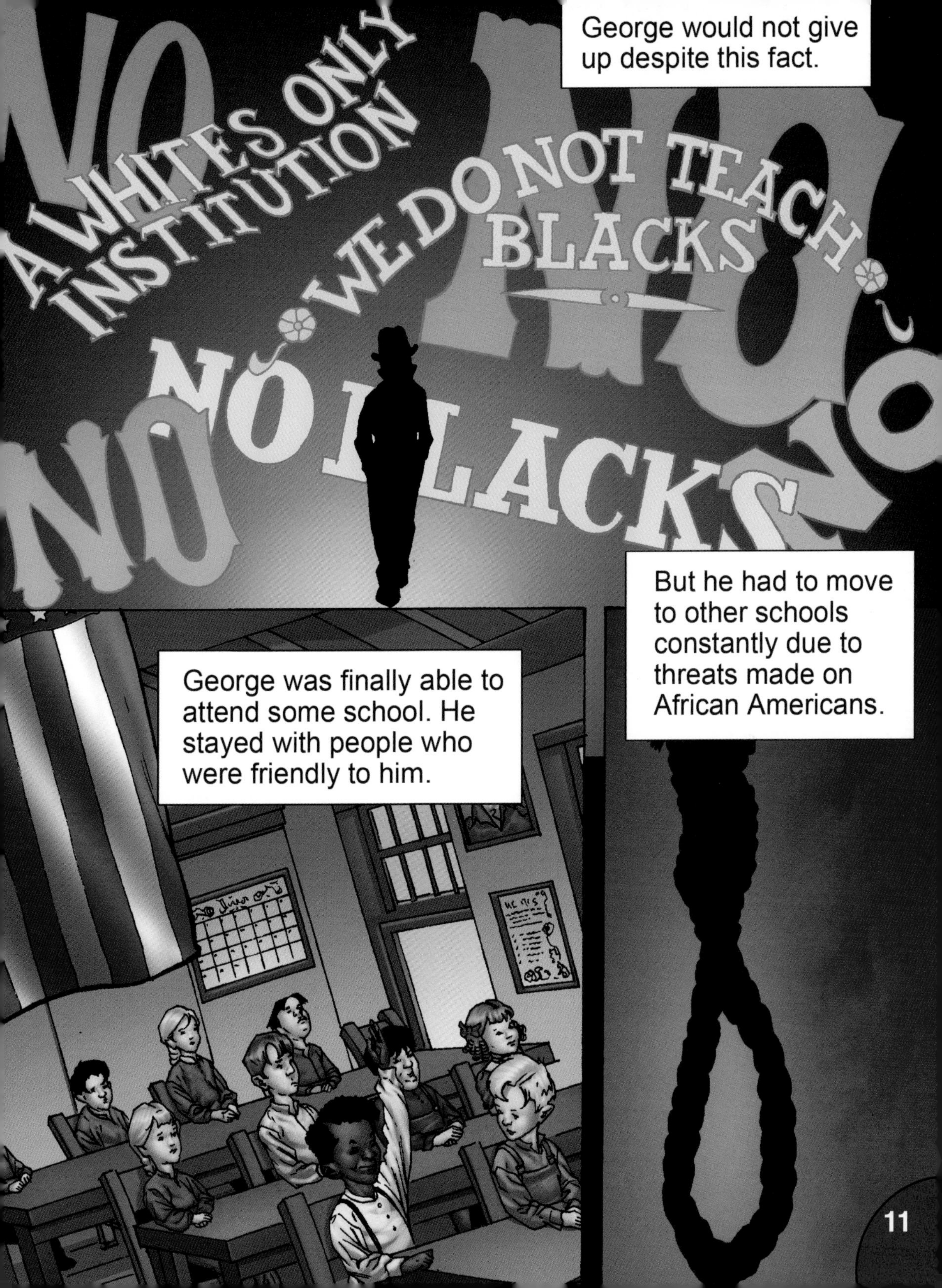
George would not give up despite this fact.
A WHITES ONLY INSTITUTION
WE DO NOT TEACH BLACKS
NO BLACKS
NO
George was finally able to attend some school. He stayed with people who were friendly to him.
But he had to move to other schools constantly due to threats made on African Americans.

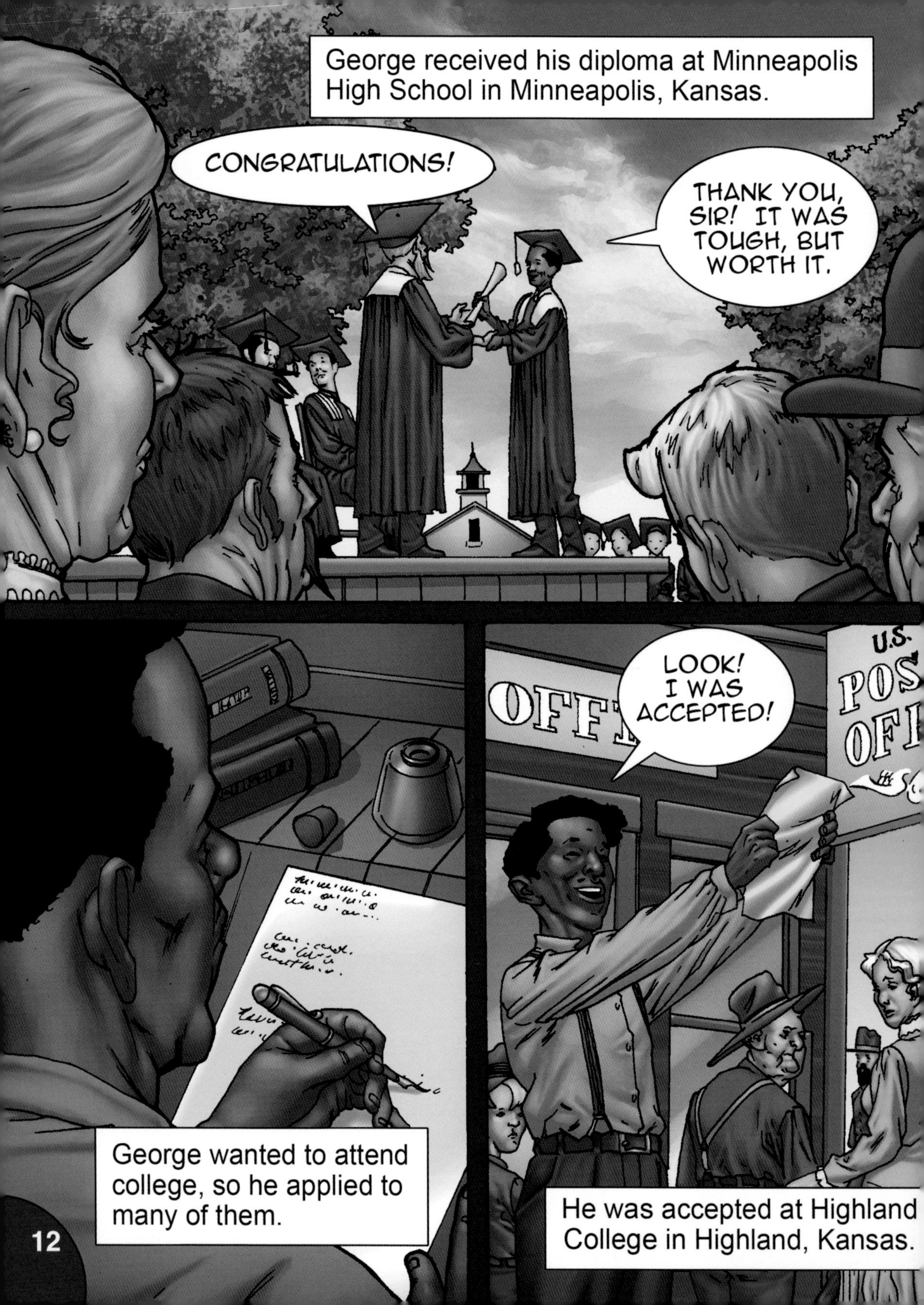
George received his diploma at Minneapolis High School in Minneapolis, Kansas.
CONGRATULATIONS!
THANK YOU, SIR! IT WAS TOUGH, BUT WORTH IT.
George wanted to attend college, so he applied to many of them.
LOOK! I WAS ACCEPTED!
U.S.
He was accepted at Highland College in Highland, Kansas.

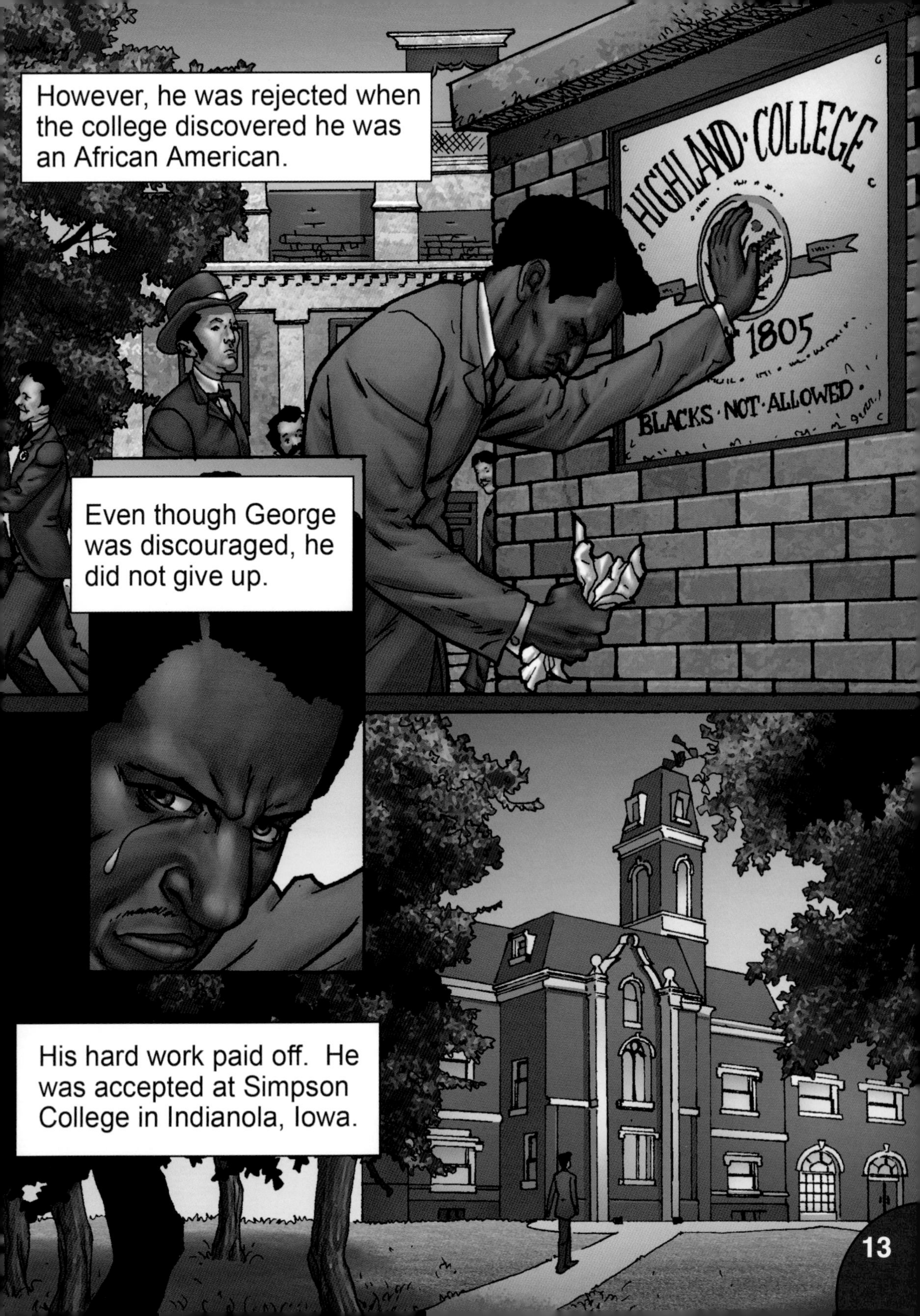
However, he was rejected when the college discovered he was an African American.
HIGHLAND·COLLEGE
1805
BLACKS·NOT·ALLOWED·
Even though George was discouraged, he did not give up.
His hard work paid off. He was accepted at Simpson College in Indianola, Iowa.

Chapter 3 Student and Teacher

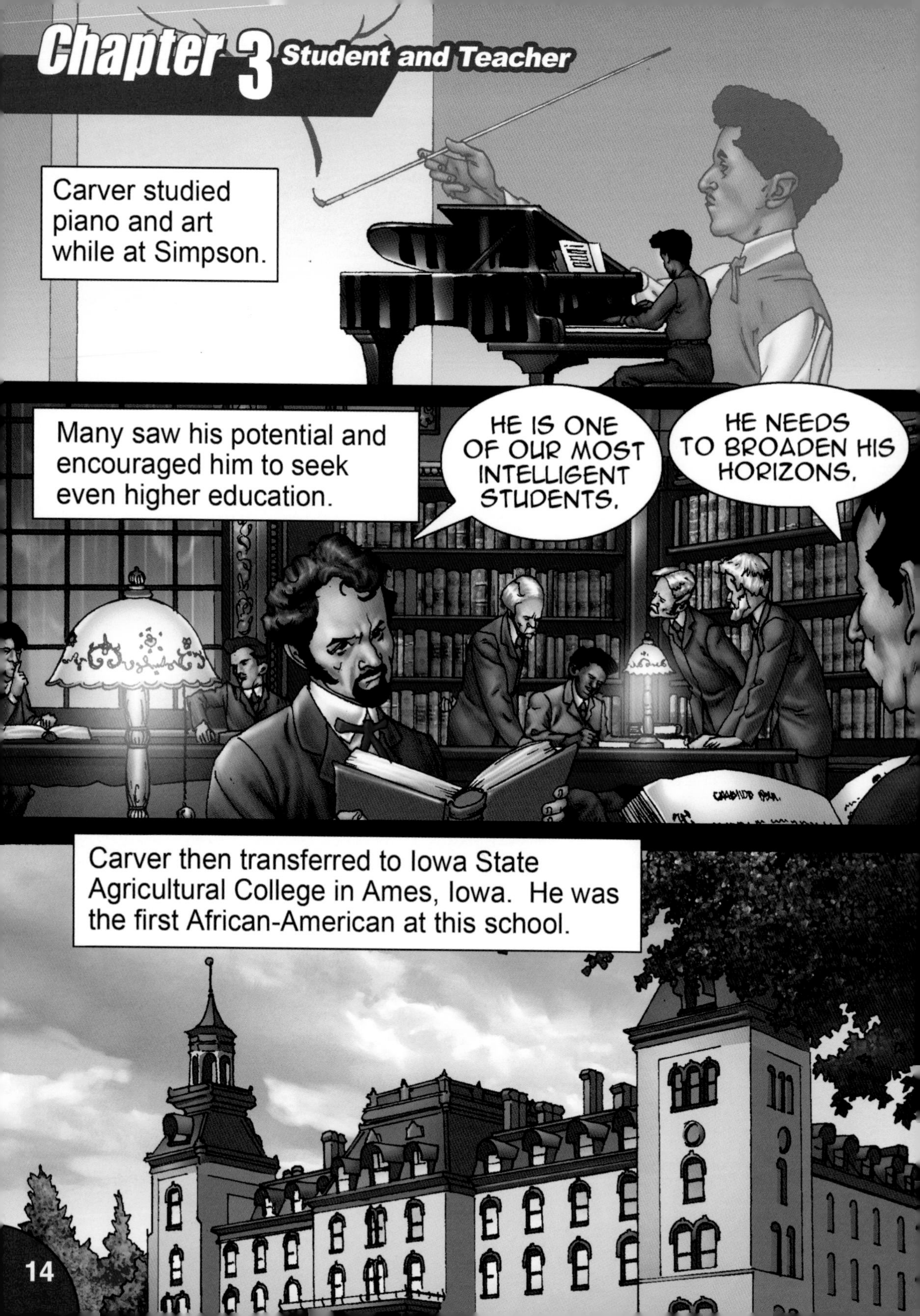
Carver studied piano and art while at Simpson.
Many saw his potential and encouraged him to seek even higher education.
HE IS ONE OF OUR MOST INTELLIGENT STUDENTS.
HE NEEDS TO BROADEN HIS HORIZONS.
Carver then transferred to Iowa State Agricultural College in Ames, Iowa. He was the first African-American at this school.

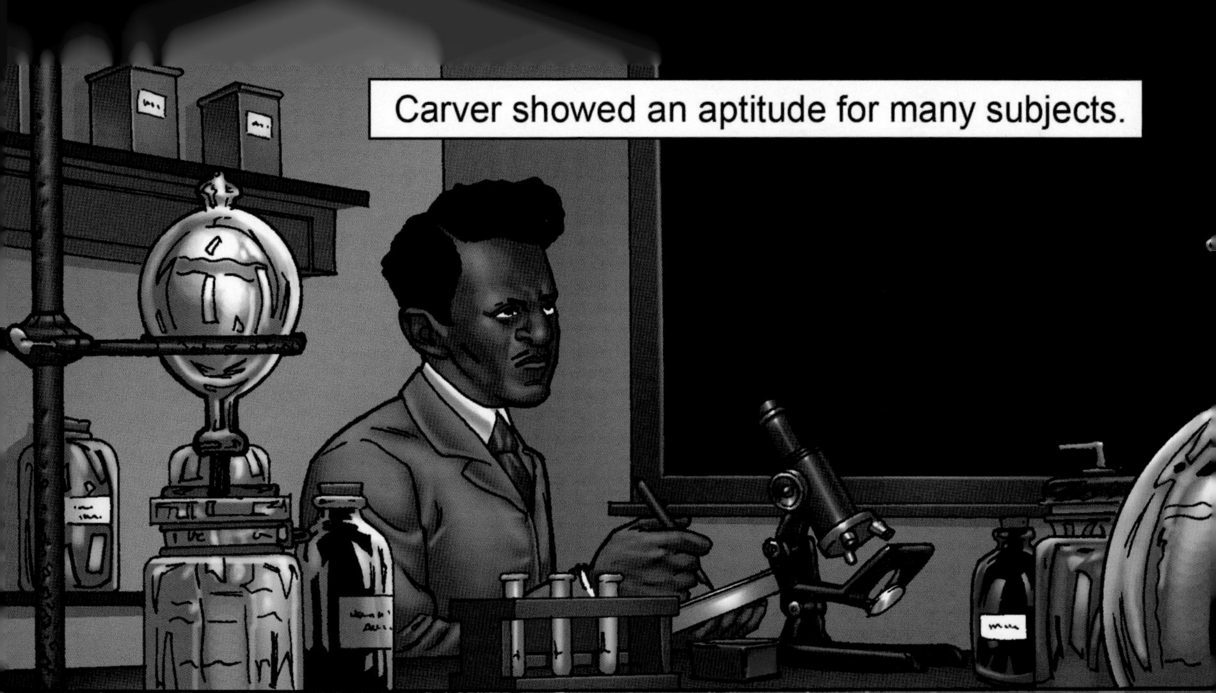
Carver showed an aptitude for many subjects.

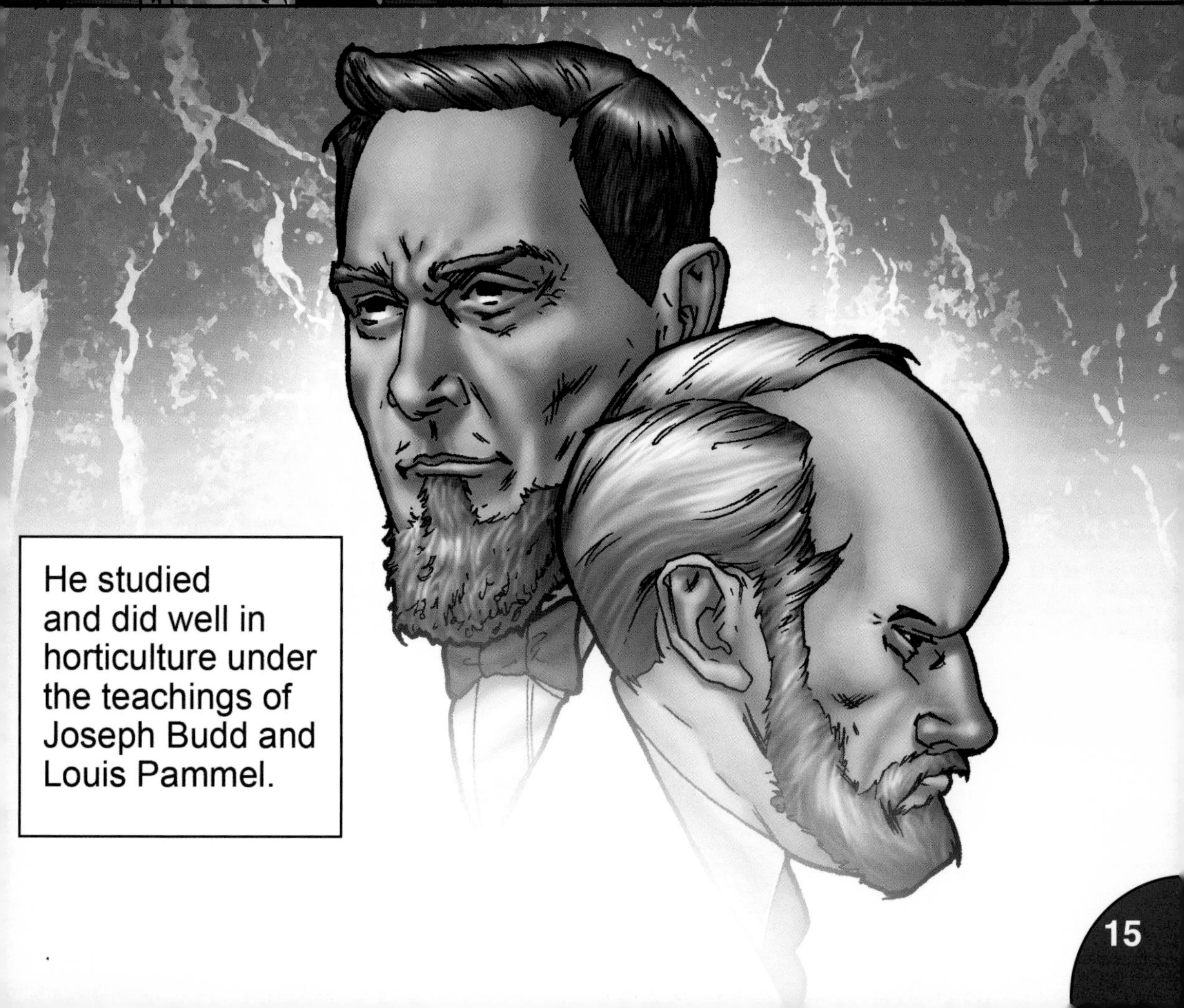
He studied
and did well in
horticulture under
the teachings of
Joseph Budd and
Louis Pammel.

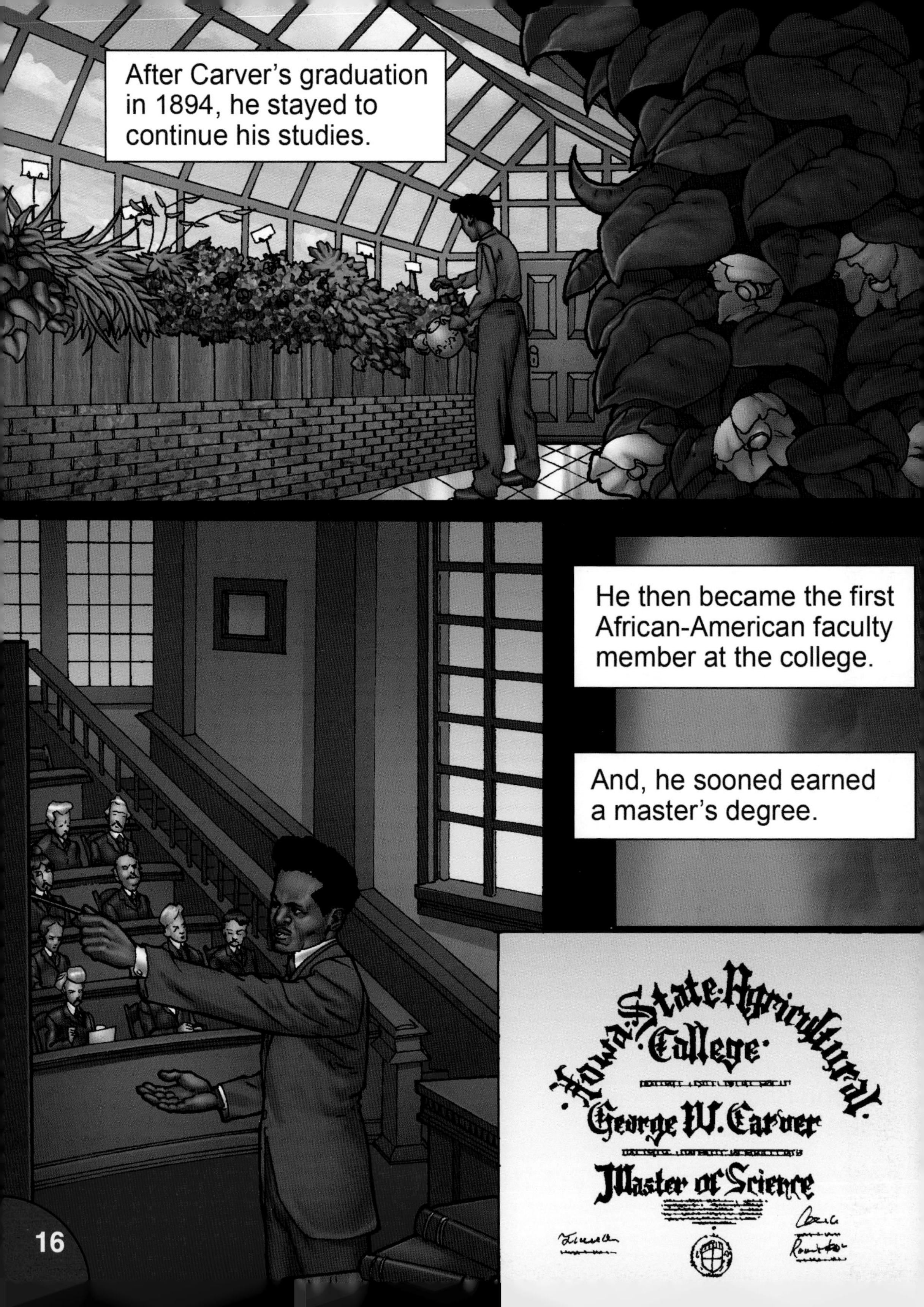
After Carver's graduation in 1894, he stayed to continue his studies.
He then became the first African-American faculty member at the college.
And, he sooned earned a master's degree.
Iowa State Agricultural College
George W. Carver
Master of Science

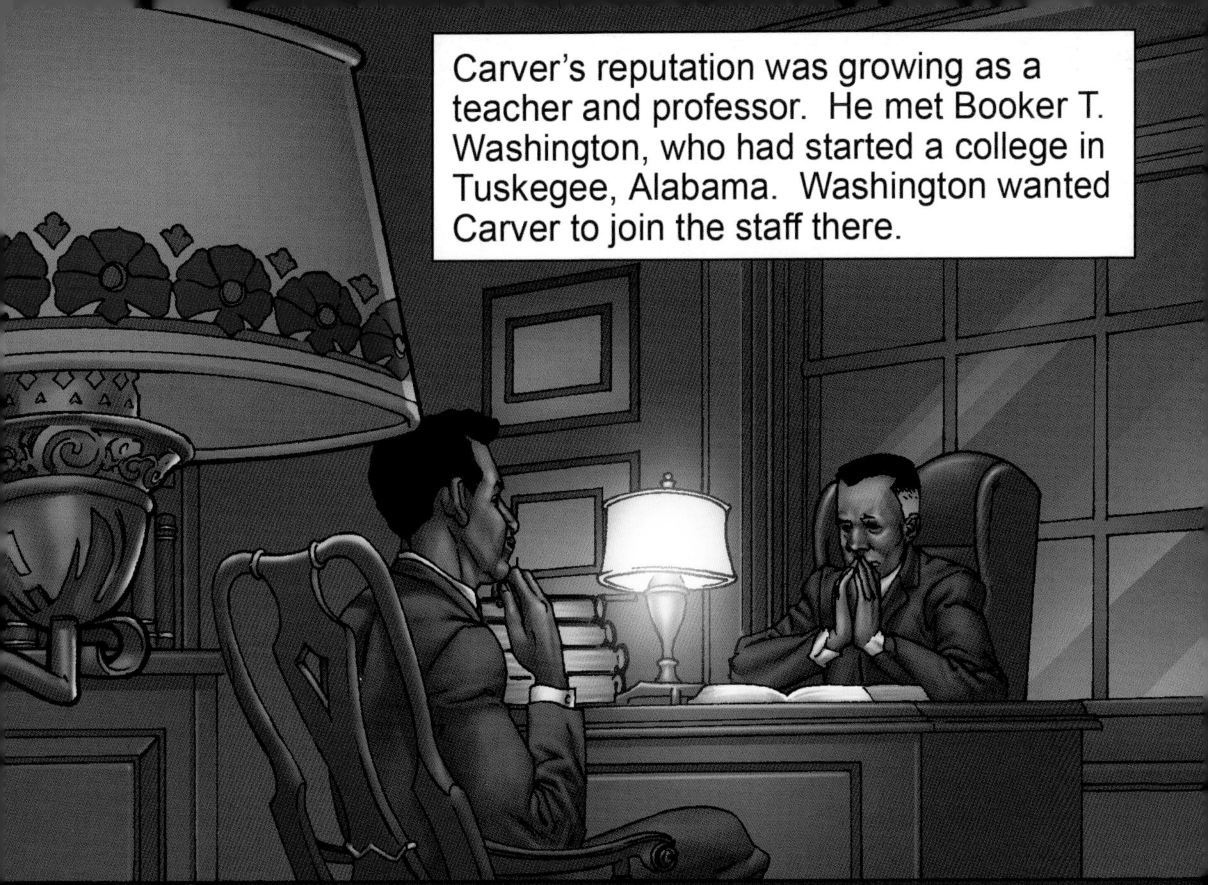
Carver's reputation was growing as a teacher and professor. He met Booker T. Washington, who had started a college in Tuskegee, Alabama. Washington wanted Carver to join the staff there.

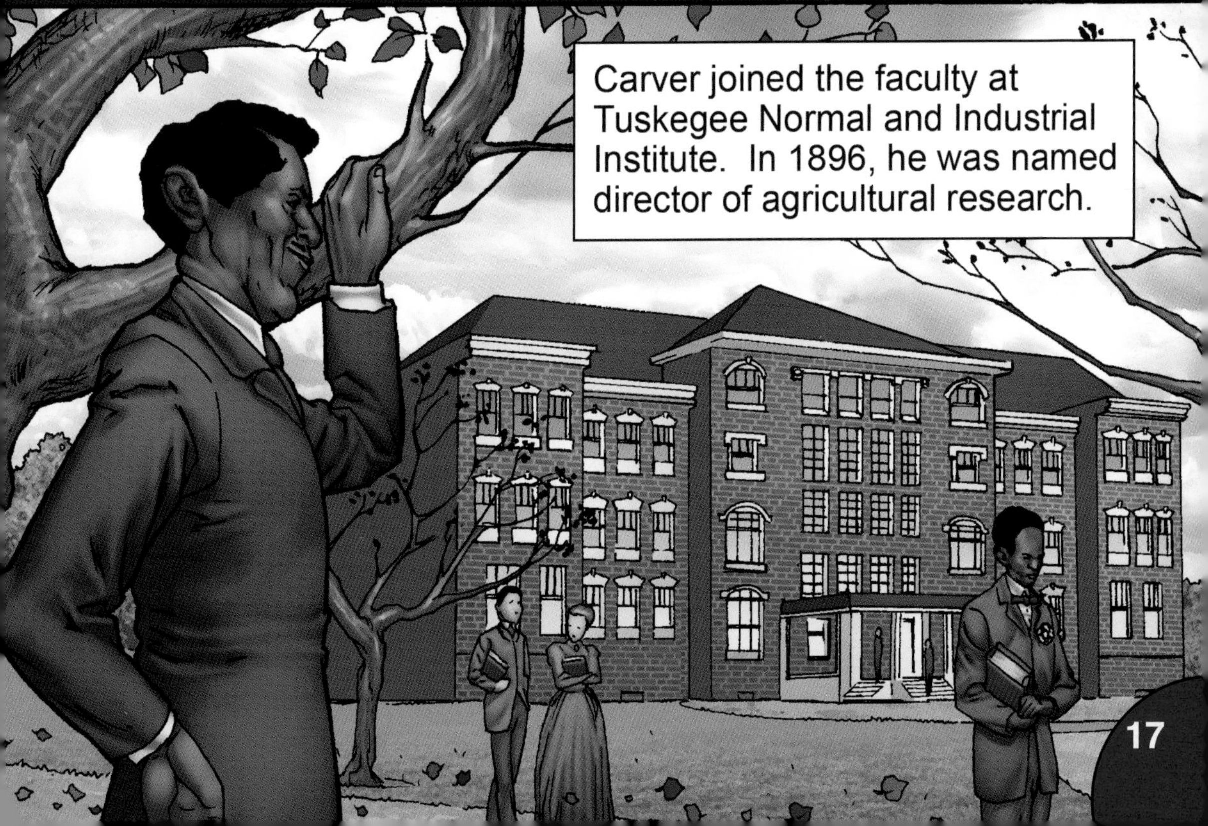
Carver joined the faculty at Tuskegee Normal and Industrial Institute. In 1896, he was named director of agricultural research.

Chapter 4 Crop Rotation

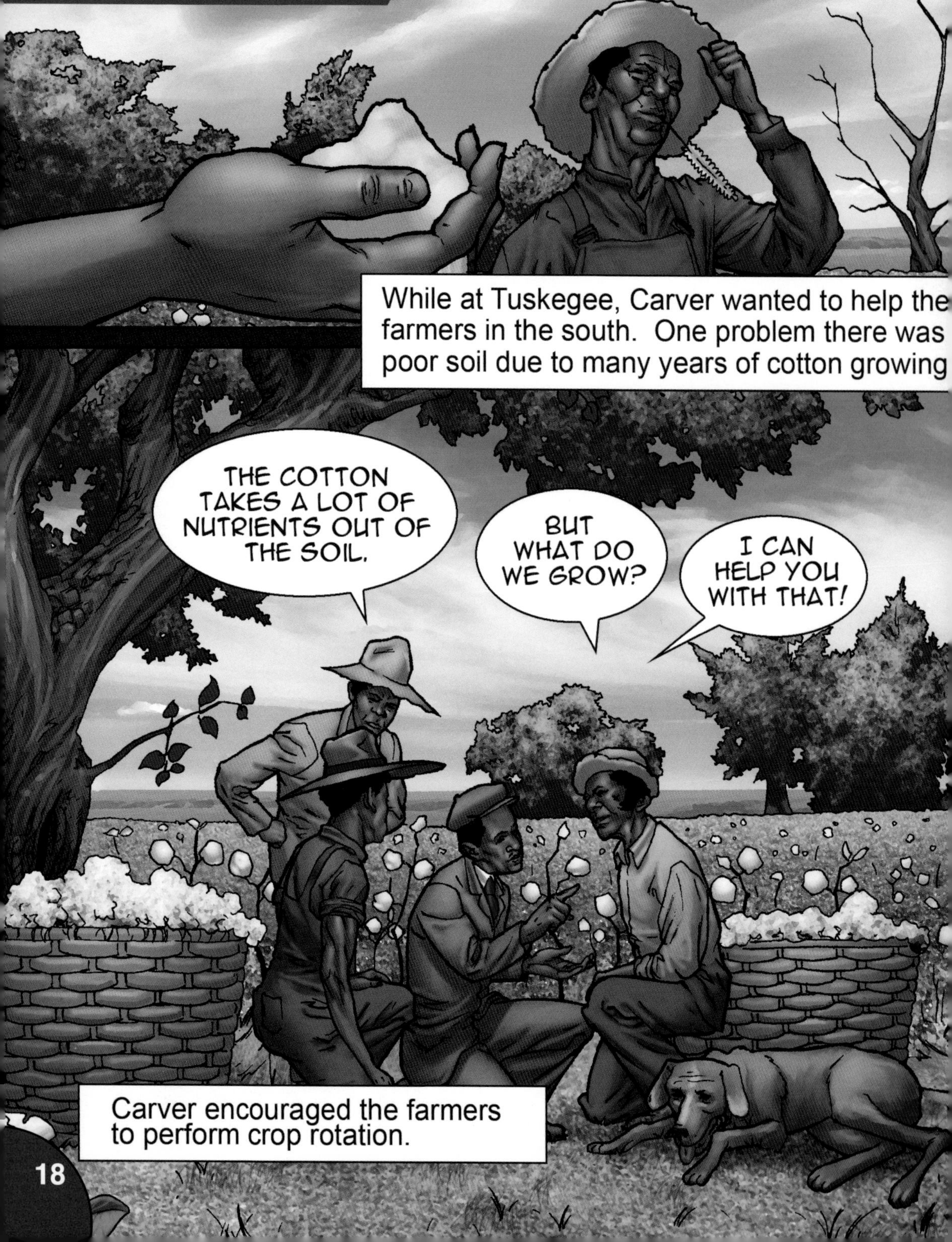
While at Tuskegee, Carver wanted to help the farmers in the south. One problem there was poor soil due to many years of cotton growing
THE COTTON TAKES A LOT OF NUTRIENTS OUT OF THE SOIL.
BUT WHAT DO WE GROW?
I CAN HELP YOU WITH THAT!
Carver encouraged the farmers to perform crop rotation.

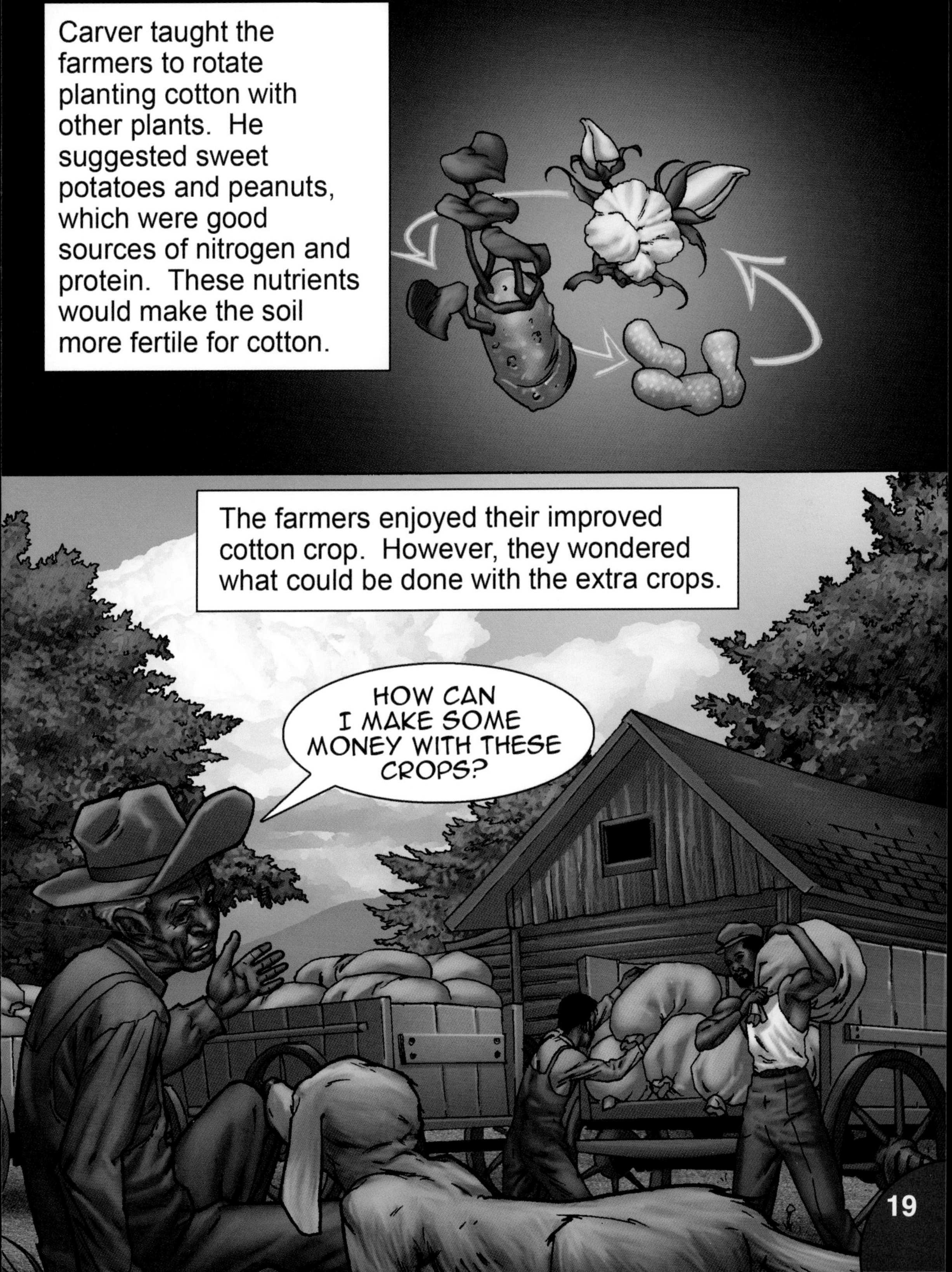
Carver taught the farmers to rotate planting cotton with other plants. He suggested sweet potatoes and peanuts, which were good sources of nitrogen and protein. These nutrients would make the soil more fertile for cotton.
The farmers enjoyed their improved cotton crop. However, they wondered what could be done with the extra crops.
HOW CAN I MAKE SOME MONEY WITH THESE CROPS?

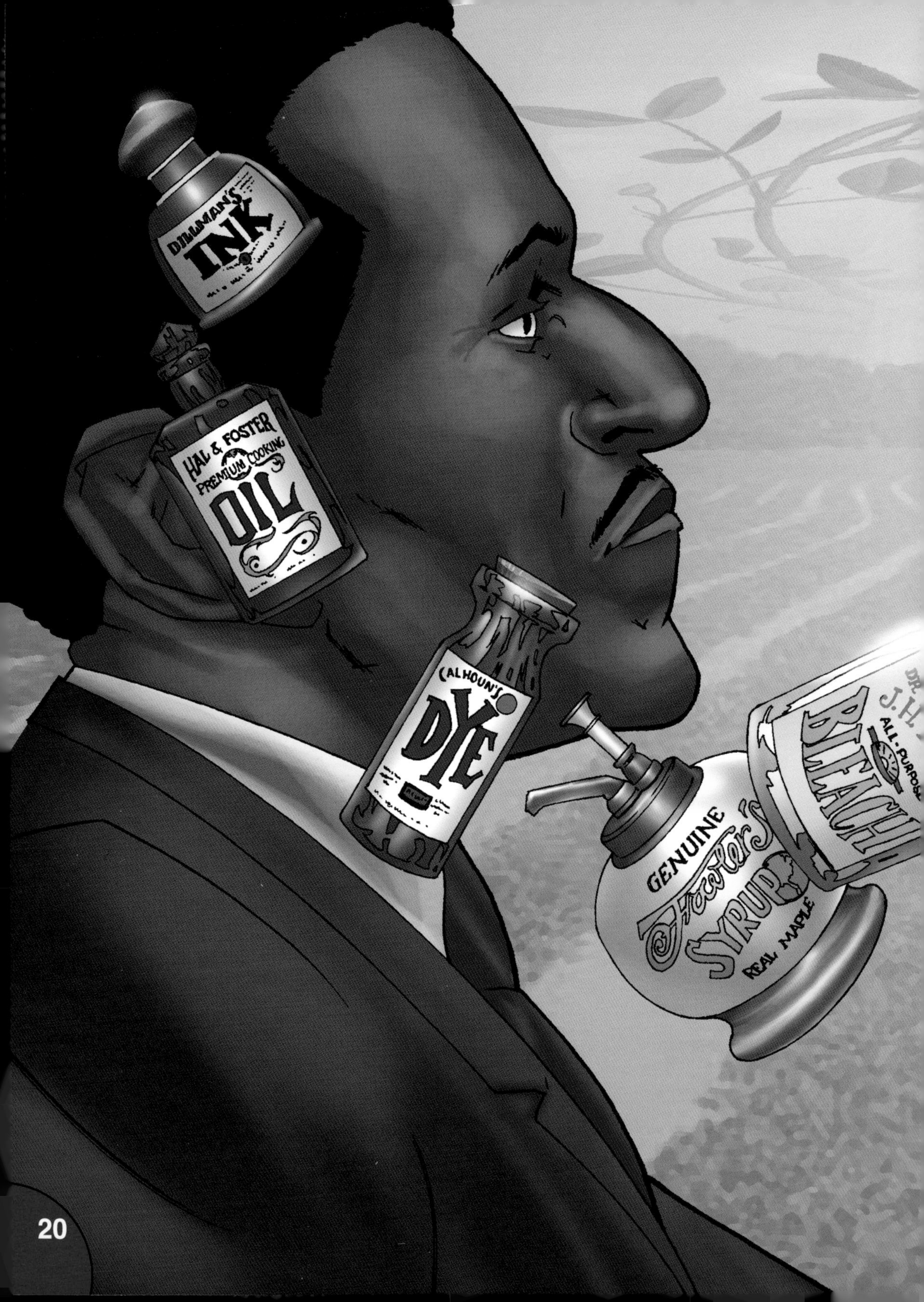
DILLMAN'S INK
HAL & FOSTER PREMIUM COOKING OIL
CALHOUN'S DYE
GENUINE Foster's SYRUP REAL MAPLE
DR. J.H.
ALL-PURPOSE BLEACH

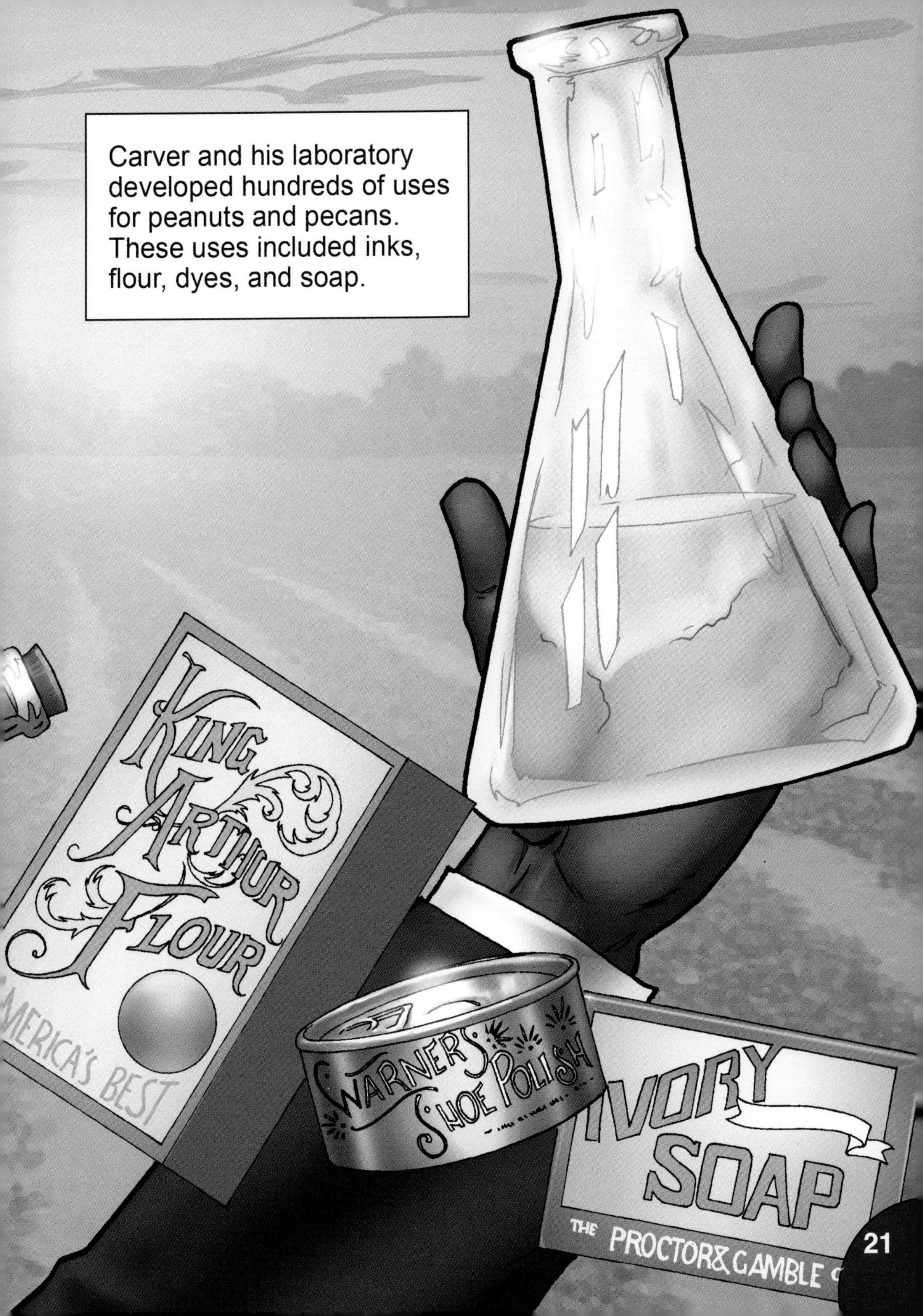
Carver and his laboratory developed hundreds of uses for peanuts and pecans. These uses included inks, flour, dyes, and soap.
KING ARTHUR FLOUR
MERICA'S BEST
WARNERS SHOE POLISH
IVORY SOAP
THE PROCTOR&GAMBLE C

Chapter 5 Presidential Adviser

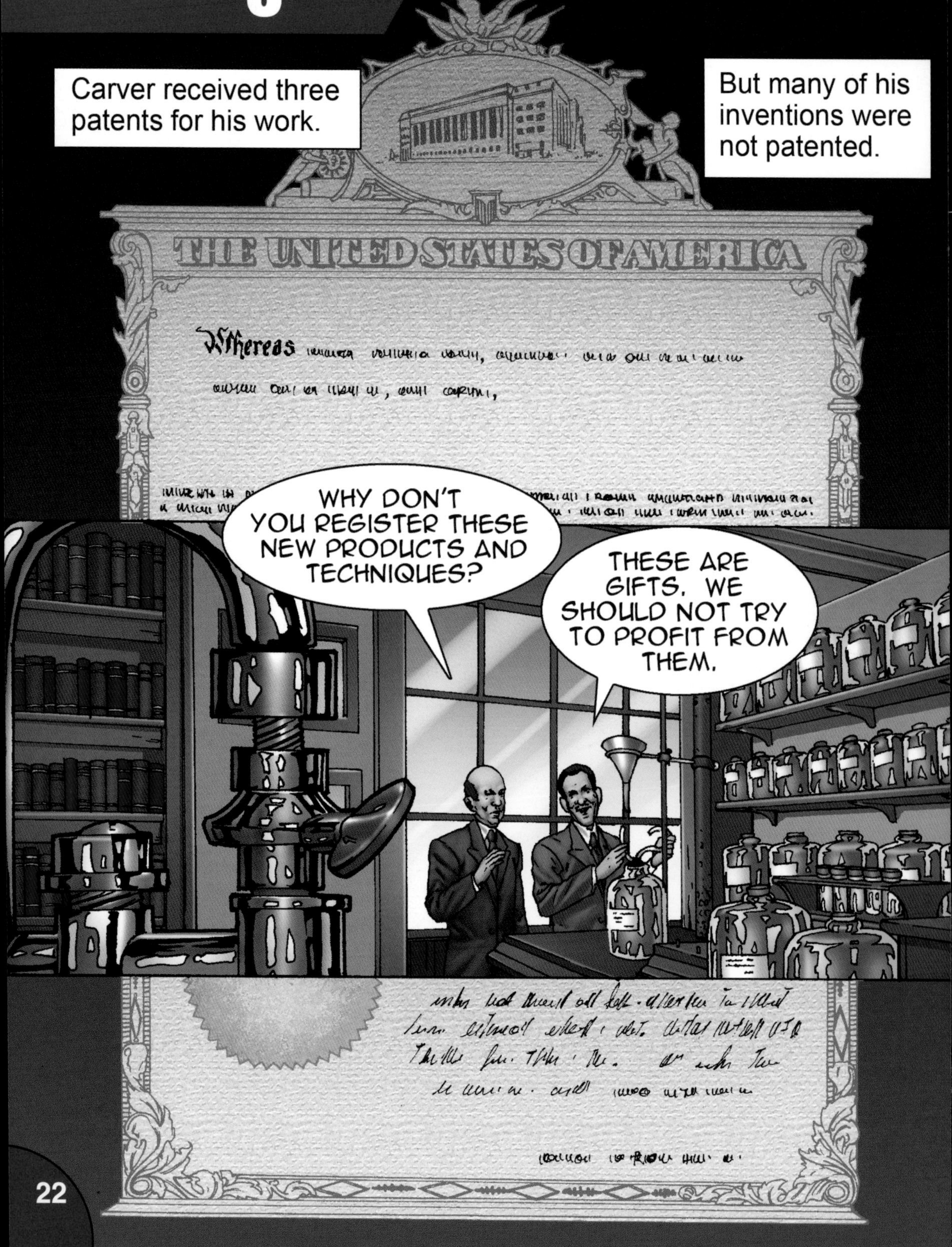
Carver received three patents for his work.
But many of his inventions were not patented.
THE UNITED STATES OF AMERICA
Whereas
WHY DON'T YOU REGISTER THESE NEW PRODUCTS AND TECHNIQUES?
THESE ARE GIFTS. WE SHOULD NOT TRY TO PROFIT FROM THEM.

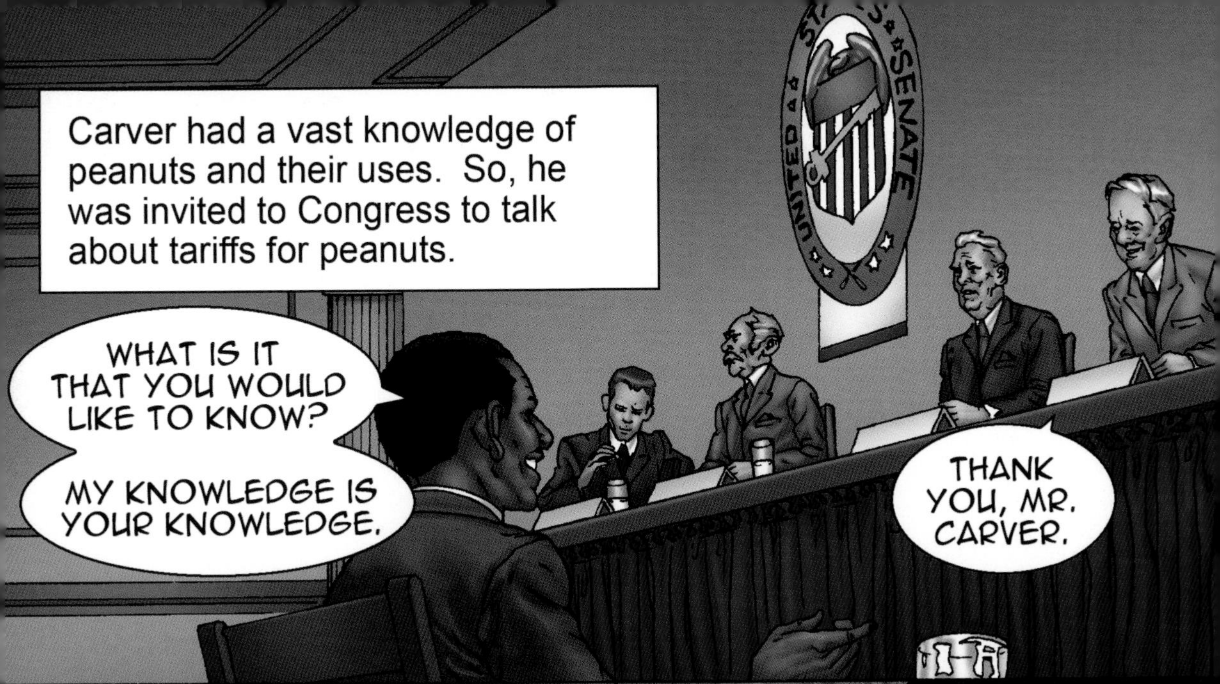
Carver had a vast knowledge of peanuts and their uses. So, he was invited to Congress to talk about tariffs for peanuts.
WHAT IS IT THAT YOU WOULD LIKE TO KNOW?
MY KNOWLEDGE IS YOUR KNOWLEDGE.
THANK YOU, MR. CARVER.

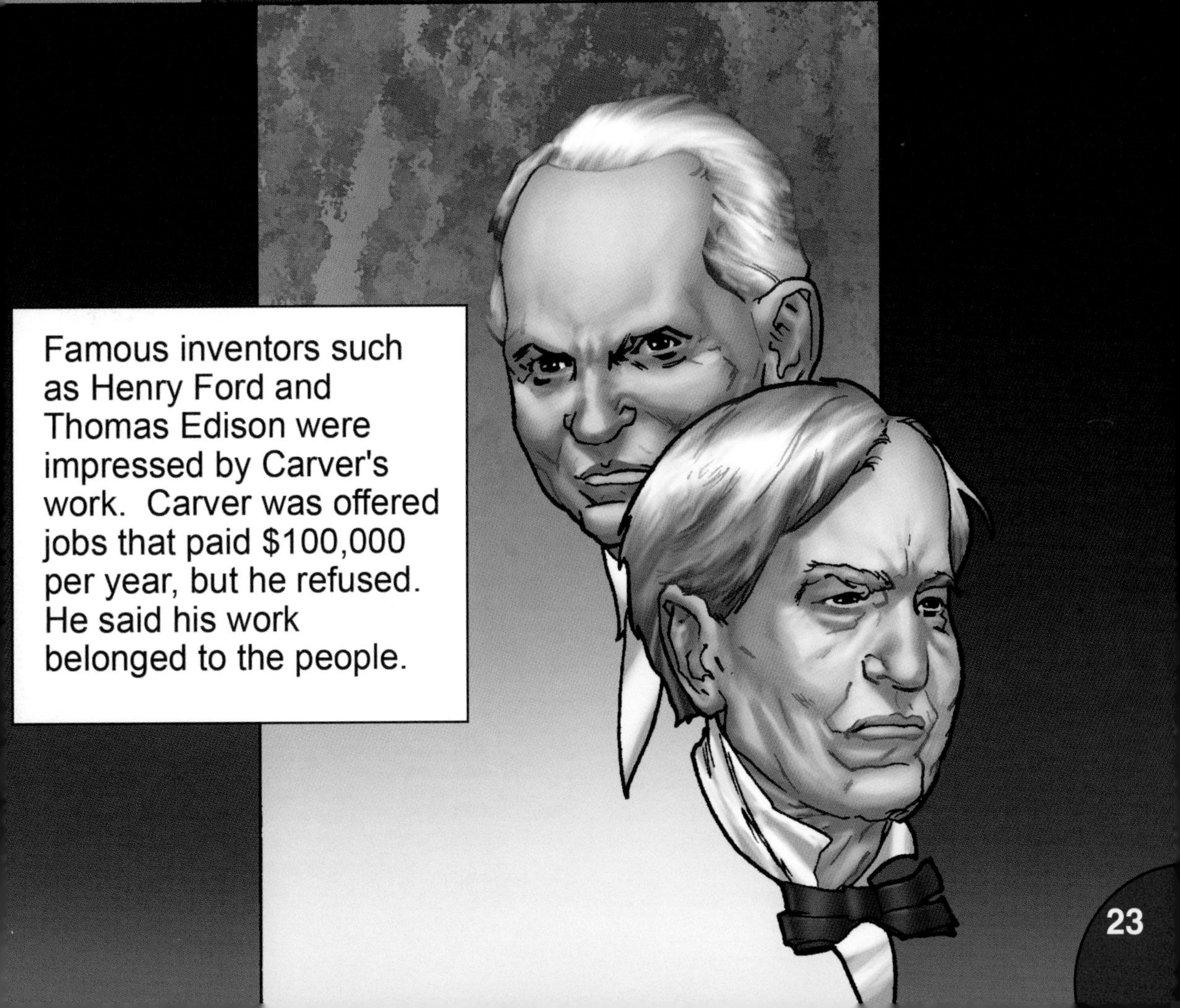
Famous inventors such as Henry Ford and Thomas Edison were impressed by Carver's work. Carver was offered jobs that paid $100,000 per year, but he refused. He said his work belonged to the people.

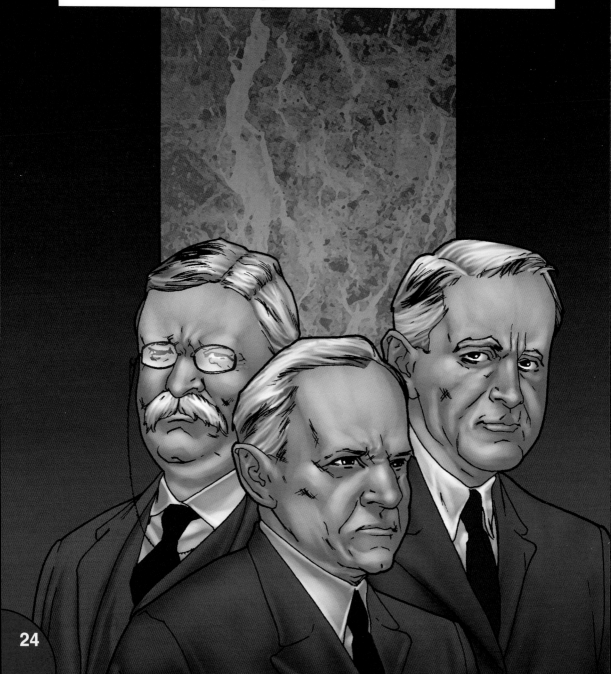

Carver continued to act as a consultant. He met with three presidents: Theodore Roosevelt, Calvin Coolidge, and Franklin Roosevelt. He gave his advice for free.

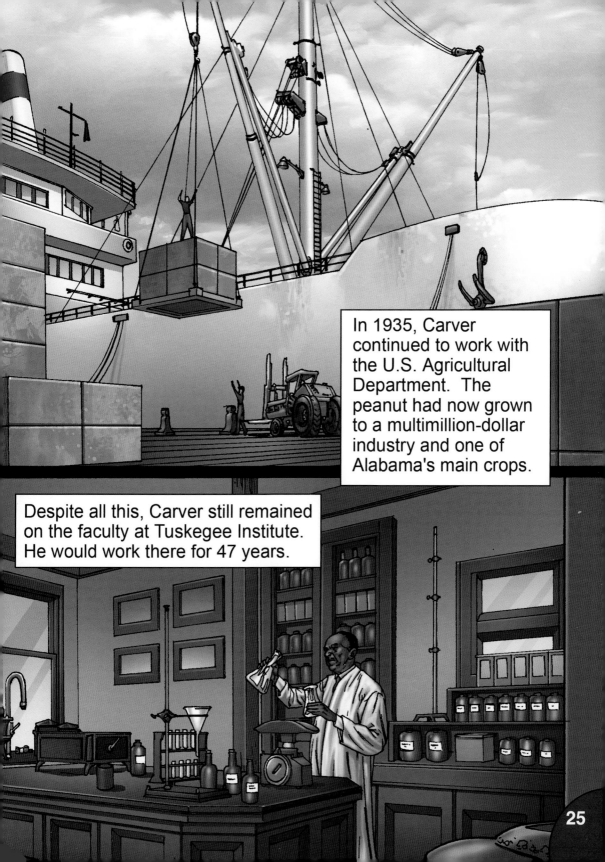

In 1935, Carver continued to work with the U.S. Agricultural Department. The peanut had now grown to a multimillion-dollar industry and one of Alabama's main crops.

Despite all this, Carver still remained on the faculty at Tuskegee Institute. He would work there for 47 years.

Chapter 6 Continuing His Life's Work

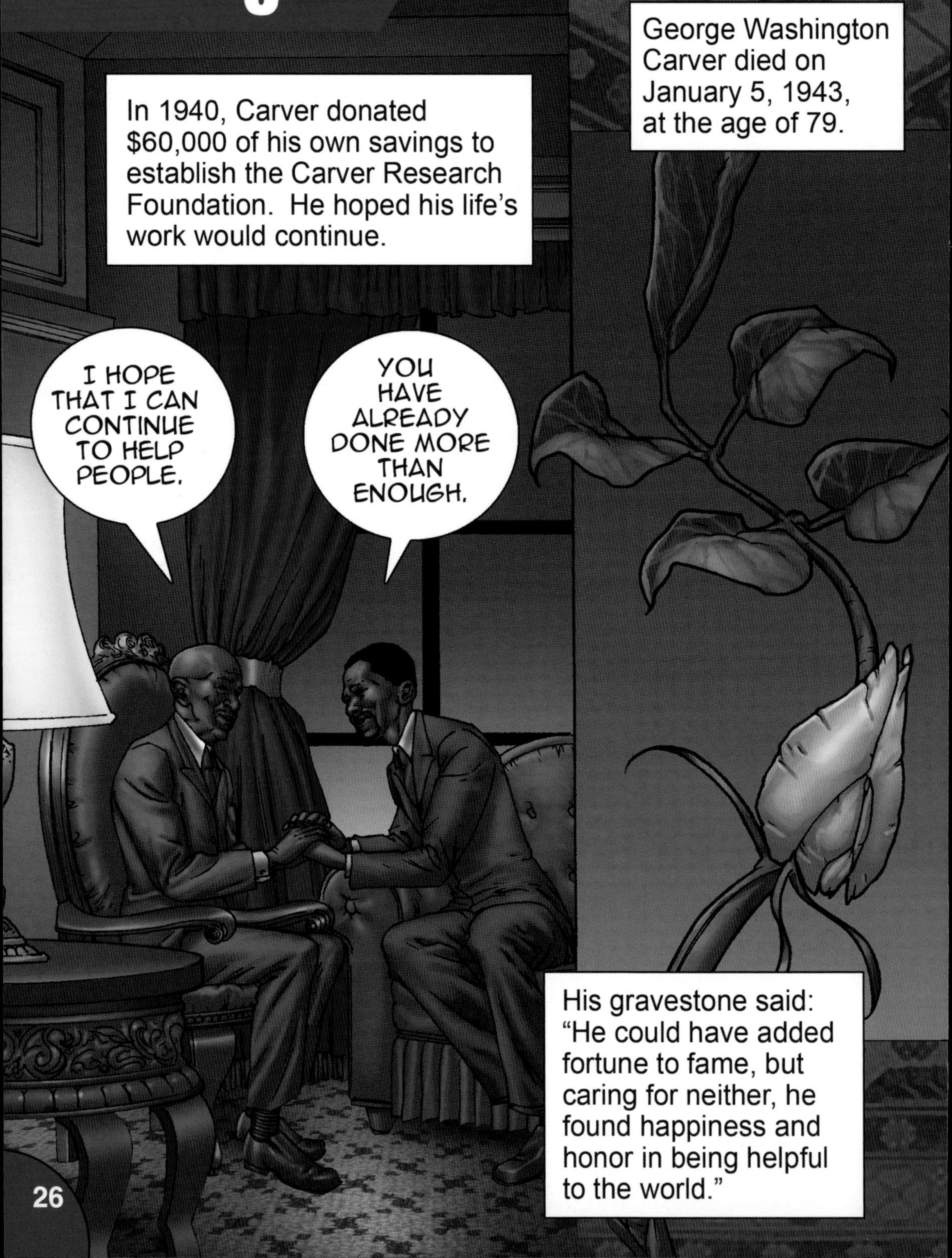

In 1940, Carver donated $60,000 of his own savings to establish the Carver Research Foundation. He hoped his life's work would continue.
I HOPE THAT I CAN CONTINUE TO HELP PEOPLE.
YOU HAVE ALREADY DONE MORE THAN ENOUGH.
George Washington Carver died on January 5, 1943, at the age of 79.
His gravestone said: "He could have added fortune to fame, but caring for neither, he found happiness and honor in being helpful to the world."

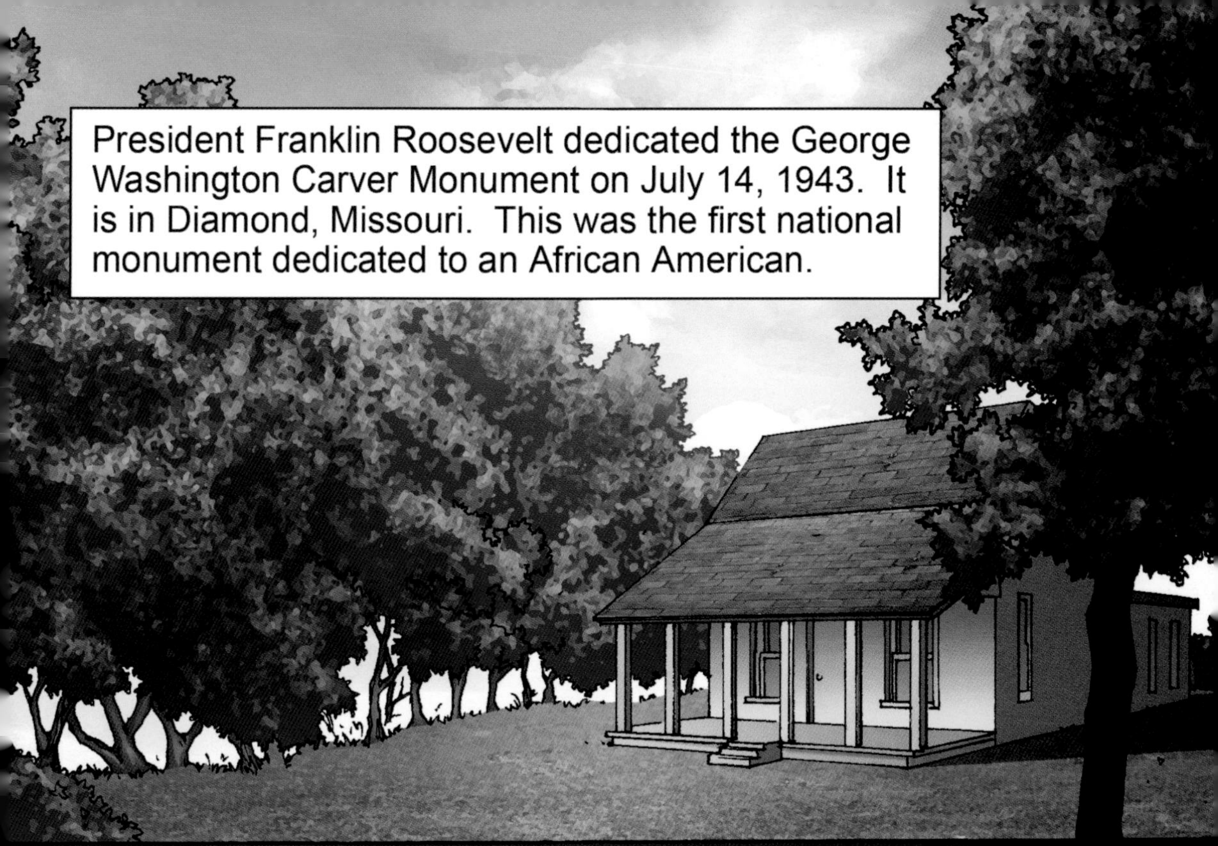
President Franklin Roosevelt dedicated the George Washington Carver Monument on July 14, 1943. It is in Diamond, Missouri. This was the first national monument dedicated to an African American.

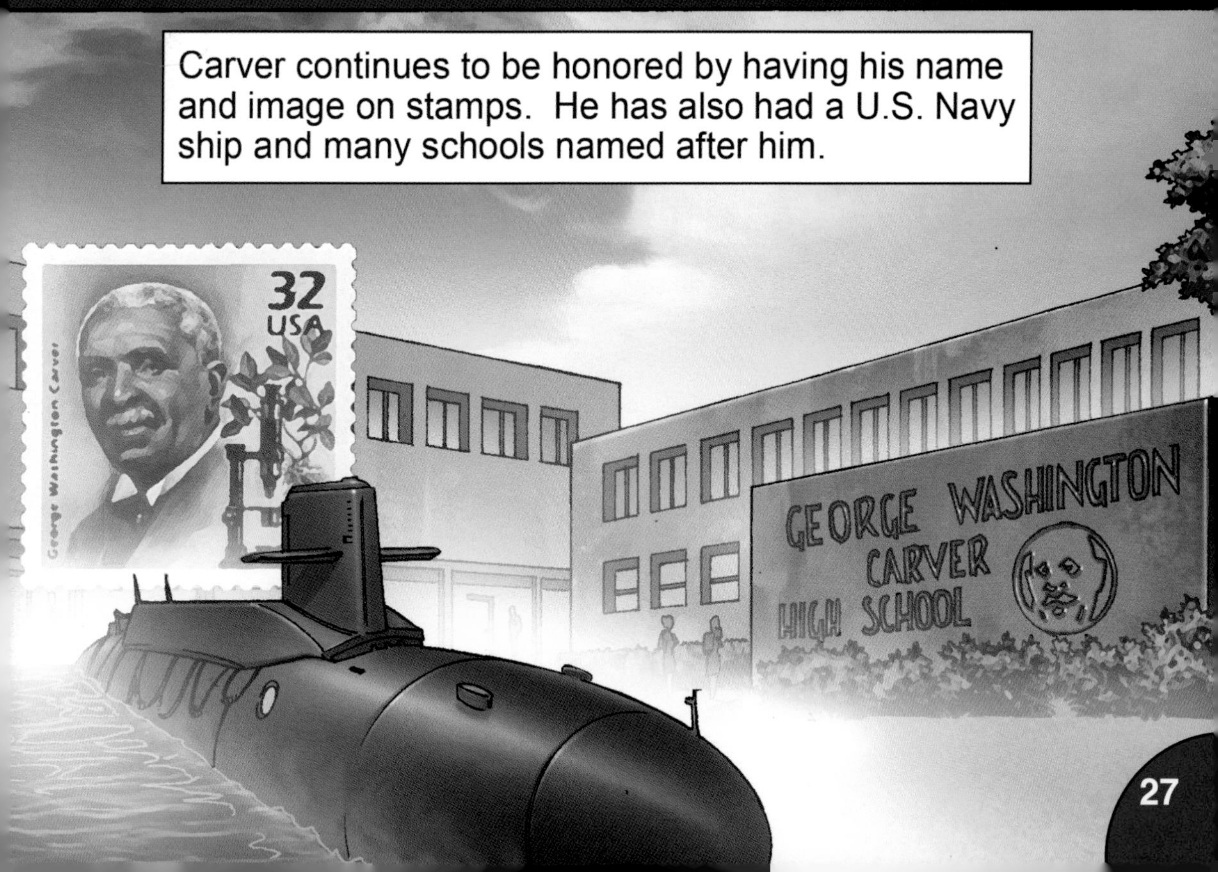
Carver continues to be honored by having his name and image on stamps. He has also had a U.S. Navy ship and many schools named after him.
32
USA
George Washington Carver
GEORGE WASHINGTON
CARVER
HIGH SCHOOL

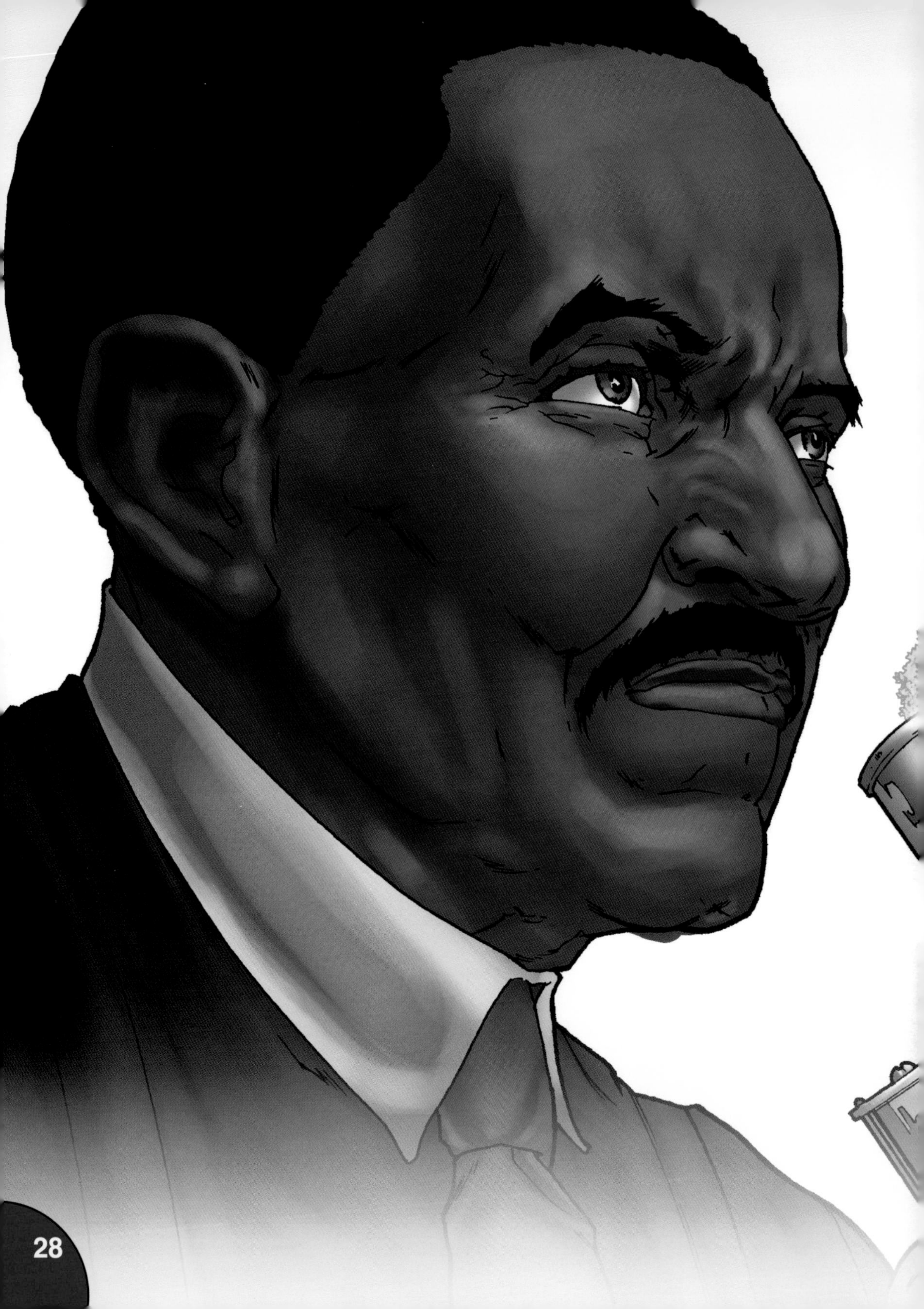

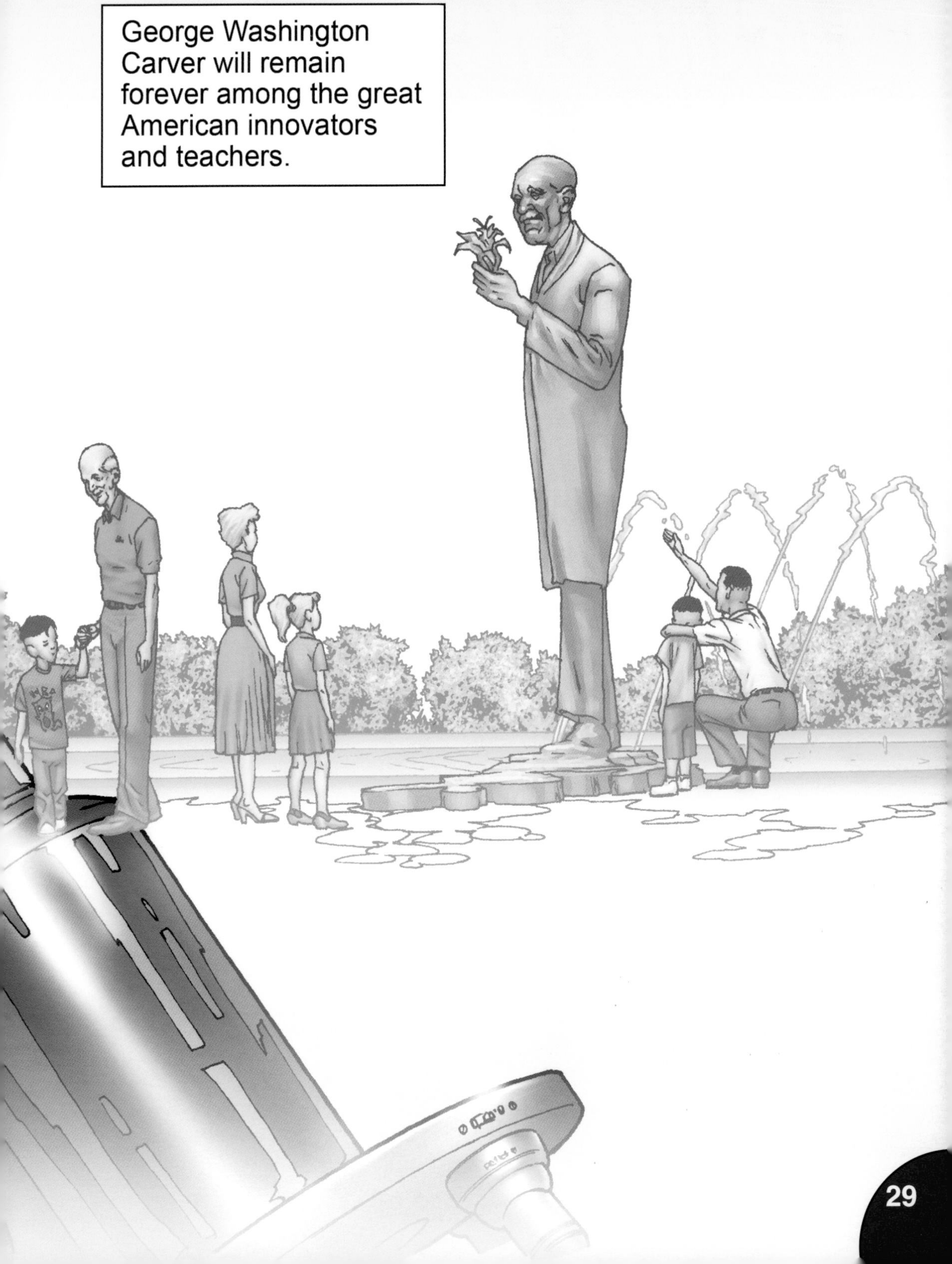
George Washington Carver will remain forever among the great American innovators and teachers.

Further Reading

Carey, Charles W. Jr. *George Washington Carver.* Journey to Freedom. Eden Prairie: Child's World Inc., 1999.

MacLeod, Elizabeth. *George Washington Carver: An Innovative Life.* Toronto: Kids Can Press, 2007.

Mitchell, Barbara. *A Pocketful of Goobers: A Story about George Washington Carver.* Minneapolis: Lerner Publishing Group, 1987.

Wheeler, Jill C. *George Washington Carver.* Breaking Barriers. Edina: ABDO Publishing Company, 2003.

Glossary

aptitude - a natural ability, especially for learning new things.

civil war - a war between groups in the same country. The United States of America and the Confederate States of America fought a civil war from 1861 to 1865.

dedicate - to hold a ceremony that officially sets aside something for a specific use.

diploma - a document that shows graduation from school or an educational program.

fertile - able to produce plentiful crops.

horticulture - the science of growing fruits, vegetables, flowers, and other plants.

innovator - a person who develops a new idea, method, or device.

nickname - a descriptive name given to a person by friends, family, or the media.

nutrient - a substance found in plants and minerals to promote growth, maintenance, and repair.

patent - an official document giving a person the right or privilege to perform an act or a duty.

potential - capable of being or becoming. Something that is possible, but not actual.

tariff - the taxes a government puts on imported or exported goods.

Web Sites

To learn more about George Washington Carver, visit ABDO Publishing Company on the World Wide Web at **www.abdopublishing.com**. Web sites about Carver are featured on our Book Links page. These links are routinely monitored and updated to provide the most current information available.

Index